Producing Pedagogy

Producing Pedagogy

By

Lorelle Burton, Jill Lawrence,
Ann Dashwood and Alice Brown

Producing Pedagogy,
by Lorelle Burton, Jill Lawrence, Ann Dashwood and Alice Brown

This book first published 2013

Cambridge Scholars Publishing

12 Back Chapman Street, Newcastle upon Tyne, NE6 2XX, UK

British Library Cataloguing in Publication Data
A catalogue record for this book is available from the British Library

Copyright © 2013 by Lorelle Burton, Jill Lawrence, Ann Dashwood and Alice Brown

All rights for this book reserved. No part of this book may be reproduced, stored in a retrieval system, or transmitted, in any form or by any means, electronic, mechanical, photocopying, recording or otherwise, without the prior permission of the copyright owner.

ISBN (10): 1-4438-4592-2, ISBN (13): 978-1-4438-4592-2

Table of Contents

List of Figures vii

List of Tables viii

Foreword ix

Preface xii

Acknowledgements xv

Chapter One 1
The Journey: An Institutional Pedagogy in the Making
Ann Dashwood, Jill Lawrence, Lorelle Burton and Alice Brown

Chapter Two 17
Reviewing Five Key Principles of Pedagogy
Lorelle Burton, Jill Lawrence, Ann Dashwood, and Alice Brown

Chapter Three 37
Principles to Practice: Students' Learning Experiences
Lorelle Burton, Alice Brown, Ann Dashwood and Jill Lawrence

Chapter Four 54
Delving Deeper: Exploring Students' Learning Experiences of the Five Principles of Pedagogy
Jill Lawrence, Ann Dashwood, Alice Brown and Lorelle Burton

Chapter Five 74
Embracing the Richness of Student Context in Pedagogy
Alice Brown, Ann Dashwood, Jill Lawrence and Lorelle Burton

Chapter Six 93
Exploring the Five Key Principles: Staff Perspectives
Ann Dashwood, Jill Lawrence, Alice Brown and Lorelle Burton

Chapter Seven 117
Learning from the SALT Fellowship Phase
Jill Lawrence, Ann Dashwood, Alice Brown and Lorelle Burton

Chapter Eight 139
Unravelling the Meaning of Sustainability and Flexibility for a Pedagogy
Ann Dashwood, Alice Brown, Jill Lawrence and Lorelle Burton

Chapter Nine 156
Anticipating a Responsive, Relevant and Agile Institutional Pedagogy
Jill Lawrence, Ann Dashwood, Lorelle Burton and Alice Brown

About the Authors 187

LIST OF FIGURES

Figure 6.1: Academics' perspectives on the five principles

Figure 7.1: Map illustrating SALT fellowship processes

Figure 9.1: Intersecting principles in an institutional pedagogy

LIST OF TABLES

Table 3.1: Frequencies for Age (Scaled), Faculty, and Study Location
Table 3.2: Descriptive Statistics for the Five Principle Scale Scores (N= 944)
Table 3.3: Yes/No percentages for evidence of Five Principles' application in S2 2007 courses
Table 3.4: Correlations for Five Principles with Two Background Variables (N=944)
Table 3.5: Descriptive Statistics for Importance, Frequency, and Knowledge Extension Measures
Table 4.1: Summary of Students' Responses
Table 4.2: Positive and Negative Instances of Reporting Sustainability Principle Categories
Table 4.3: Positive and Negative Instances of Reporting Engagement Principle Categories
Table 4.4: Positive and Negative Instances of Reporting Scholarship Principle Categories
Table 4.5: Positive and Negative Instances of Reporting Flexibility Principle Categories
Table 4.6: Positive and Negative Instances of Reporting Contextual Learning Principle Categories
Table 6.1: Positive Instances of Reporting Sustainability Principle Categories
Table 6.2: Positive Instances of Reporting Engagement Principle Categories
Table 6.3: Positive Instances of Reporting Scholarship Principle Categories
Table 6.4: Positive Instances of Reporting Flexibility Principle Categories
Table 6.5: Positive Instances of Reporting Contextual Learning Principle Categories
Table 7.1: Sample Matrix for Curriculum Design Module
Table 9.1: USQ's Key Organisational Goals (2008-2013)

FOREWORD

In 1963 the Western world was rocked by a scandal of unprecedented proportions. Five senior British diplomats and civil servants were charged with espionage. The five: Kim Philby, Donald Maclean, Guy Burgess, Anthony Blunt and a fifth individual whose identity remains unknown were charged with selling top secrets to the Soviet Union. Whatever success had been achieved in offsetting the problems of the Cold War suffered an immediate and immense setback with the announcement of the scandal.

What, you may be wondering, does this notorious incident have to do with a new book on pedagogical development in an Australian university?

Consider this. Philby and his co-conspirators had all attended Cambridge University, where they became acquainted with each other and in fact became known in later years as the "Cambridge Five".

And consider this. The most fundamental Cambridge value is *Freedom of thought and expression*. And the uppermost Cambridge educational principle is, *The encouragement of a questioning spirit*. All Cambridge Dons are expected to emphasise this particular value and associated educational principle in their teaching, and all Cambridge students are expected to demonstrate their essence in their learning.

Indeed, Philby credited his Cambridge experience with the development of his intense questioning of Western liberal democracy and his orientation to subversive political expression. Such, it would seem, is the remarkable potency of a centre for advanced thought when its leaders make a decision about how teaching and learning should be undertaken and its academics follow through in authentic ways in their pedagogical methods.

Consideration of this rather colourful Cambridge exemplar is incomplete without a final footnote. The University Board of Governors might well have backed away, following 1963, from a pedagogical philosophy that seemingly brought embarrassment, if not the hint of disgrace, to one of the world's most venerable institutions. But they did not. Indeed, Cambridge has gone from strength to strength in the ensuing decades and is currently ranked by some agencies as the world's leading university. And its core *Freedom of Thought and Expression* value and its *Questioning Spirit* educational principle remain very firmly intact, with an expectation that they will shape the teaching of all academics and the learning of all students.

Most modern institutes for higher learning, including Australia's 40 universities, have traditionally lacked whatever it takes to develop a highly meaningful vision and then transpose that vision into pedagogical practices à la Cambridge. Rather, the norm for most universities has seemed to be: use a PR company to develop a slick vision that has presumed marketing power and leave it to individual academics to teach in accordance with their individual capabilities, whatever they may be. And why not? The development, and implementation, of an institutional pedagogy out of a pedagogically-driven University vision statement invariably requires that academics give up a degree of their scholarly freedom and that they work collaboratively, across discipline boundaries, to develop university-wide pedagogical principles that are grounded more in the need of their University than in their individual specialisations and interests. Very few Vice Chancellors and University Councils, in my experience, are prepared to undertake such a massive developmental challenge.

Moreover, of course, there is the "Cambridge question" – Why impose a pedagogical framework on an entire university when, if you get it wrong, you can do untold damage? Much less dangerous, surely, to just let your academics do their own thing. Your university may never become a Cambridge or Harvard, but life will be peaceful.

Which brings me to this book. It is an historical account. It is a research analysis. It is a multi-biographical narrative. It is a pronouncement of educational philosophy. It is in fact all of these things, and perhaps more since it captures with remarkable clarity an event, in longitudinal perspective, that is quite remarkably unique. All in all, it is an extraordinary book.

Perhaps more than anything else, the book reveals something of the true meaning and importance of scholarly collaboration in an Australian setting. The four University of Southern Queensland co-authors were involved in the initial decision, in 2005, to give pedagogical meaning to their University's visionary construct of "transnational". They were involved in the developmental processes of the Mission taken up by the Vice Chancellor but made difficult through the retirement of senior administrators and later myself. They organised and conducted the significant research initiatives into the outcomes of earlier developmental work; and they wrote, validated and edited the chapters that follow. Their undertaking was massive and surely could not have been achieved without the highest level of mutual respect and trust. No doubt they are all much better professionals, colleagues and friends for this experience.

Let me comment also on some of the five pedagogical principles that emerged from exploration of the University's *Transnational* vision: *Sustainability; Flexibility; Scholarship; Engagement; Context.*

On the surface, these five principles would appear to lack the potential cognitive and affective impact of, say, Cambridge's *Questioning Spirit.* But a pedagogical framework that demands of academics that they think about, and nurture, *Sustainability* is surely extremely provoking in any university context; but especially so in a conservative environment such as Toowoomba, where huge demographic changes are underway – partly as a result of African refugee settlements- and a number of global and national energy industries have their headquarters. But there is more. Currently about 25%, 6500 of the university's 27000 students, are international, mostly studying online at a distance. A pedagogical principle such as *Context,* once endorsed for institution-wide usage, imposes expectations on lecturers in the first instance and students from around the world in the second instance that must surely nurture heightened thought, deepened values analysis and enriched cross-cultural relationships. One can only conclude, therefore, that what USQ has achieved, and what the four authors have captured, is a level of scholarly depth that may well be unique in contemporary Australian universities.

Finally, the book is both a beautifully written narrative and a highly credible research report. The consistency of the writing style across chapters is very impressive, given the size of the writing team. But equally impressive is the powerful data base, gained mainly from carefully constructed surveys and personal narratives. What emerges is a strong support for the fundamental construct of University-wide pedagogy, based on the perceptions of staff and students that might be regarded as surprising if it weren't so convincing.

Because of my involvement in 2005 with the origins of the USQ Transnational Pedagogy Project in my role as a Pro-Vice-Chancellor (Regional Engagement & Social Justice), I have a special interest in this publication. But the Project belongs to the authors of this book, just as much as the book itself does.

To the authors, one and all-Australian universities aren't usually known for their innovative pedagogical practice. But you have shown that there is indeed an ingenious side to the work of at least one of our higher education institutes, namely the University of Southern Queensland. You have shown that intense scholarly analysis, authentic ingenuity and rich collaboration are alive and well. Congratulations. You are an inspiration.

—Emeritus Professor Frank Crowther, AM.

PREFACE

Higher education globally is operating in a highly volatile context, a consequence of the rapid globalisation and intense technological change characteristic of the early 21st century. These forces challenge assumptions about work, productivity, and international demand for knowledge, skills and resources, igniting needs for highly competent and educated graduates. Then there are equity demands about wider access to higher levels of training and higher education for personal growth as well as demands to advance national goals of innovation and technology in a changing world. At the same time, levels of government scrutiny and reporting are increasing, external quality audits are in place and external pressures for change are escalating. As Geoff Scott, Hamish Coates and Michelle Anderson argue in their 2008 Australian Council of Educational Research Report, funding per capita is decreasing while competition is increasing; institutions are more commercial; students are more numerous, diverse and forthright about getting value for money paid; and concurrently, rapid developments in Information and Communication Technologies have made possible modes and approaches to learning unimagined 30 years ago. For instance, there is a proliferation of sources of education, think of the massive open online courses (MOOCs), and open educational resources (OERs),and an increasing blending of various technologies, particularly digital, in delivery, management and support.

Regional and local change forces exacerbate the current volatility. These include the need to manage the pressures for continuous change while simultaneously dealing with slow and unresponsive administrative processes. There are also challenges in finding and retaining high-quality staff, recruiting students in unpredictable economic times, meeting the requirements for increased government reporting, and balancing work and family life for both staff and students. Questions are generated about the extent to which the University is the traditional place where new knowledge is created and, according to Scott, Coates and Anderson in their preface, where learning is equated with the transmission of set content using a "one-size-fits-all" model delivered in lecture theatres, tutorials, and laboratories on a set timetable operated at the institution's convenience over fixed semesters.

To remain viable, universities have to build their capacity to respond promptly, positively and wisely to these interlaced combinations of "change forces". One answer is the instigation of an institutional learning and teaching redesign to enhance quality and promote good practice: a redesign capable of meeting future learning needs in the 21st century. However, efforts to develop capability in relation to learning and teaching vary widely across institutions. While some institutions focus on further developing individuals' knowledge and skills within their discipline, others provide an additional learning and teaching framework to build institutional knowledge and capabilities and connect them to the university's strategic plan. This book focuses on the second approach. Taking a longitudinal perspective, covering seven years and three separate research projects, the book describes the development and subsequent evaluation of a whole-of-institution approach to pedagogy.

Producing pedagogy presents nine chapters peer reviewed by esteemed colleagues and international experts in the fields of learning and teaching and higher education research and development. Chapter One sets the scene by outlining the development and adaptation of a whole-of-institution pedagogy at the University of Southern Queensland (USQ), a regional university in Queensland, Australia. The chapter explains how a project team developed the rationale for an institutional pedagogy based on five associated pedagogical principles: Sustainability, Engagement, Scholarship, Flexibility, and Contextual Learning. Chapter Two reviews the literature underpinning each of those principles.

The initial impetus to produce the pedagogy was USQ's 2005 vision to be Australia's leading transnational educator. However two years later, USQ's vision changed to an emphasis on a commitment to sustainability and flexibility. The *transnational pedagogy* became a *best practice learning and teaching pedagogy*. The research team was able to accommodate this change, as well as the others which were to follow, because of the applicability and continued relevance of the five principles in relation to USQ's strategic planning, and to the higher education literature.

Chapters Three, Four, and Five report the findings of a research study conducted to investigate the applicability of the five principles to both students and staff in the USQ context. The research process and student results are documented in ChaptersThree (the quantitative results) and Four (the qualitative results) while Chapter Five specifically investigates the students' perceptions and experiences of the Contextual Learning principle. Chapter Six discusses the staff results (both the quantitative and qualitative).

In 2010 the authors were awarded a USQ Fellowship to develop an online questionnaire, the Self-Assessment of Learning and Teaching (SALT) tool, with inbuilt sources of information and support. The online SALT platform was designed to facilitate capacity-building among USQ academic staff using the five principles as a framework. The platform enabled staff to reflect, prioritise, and develop their learning and teaching design and delivery capacities in line with the principles described in this book. Chapter Seven outlines how the fellowship project, including how the SALT platform was developed and piloted. The chapter augments understandings already developed about the efficacy of two of the five pedagogical principles–Engagement and Scholarship. Chapters Eight and Nine enhance understandings in relation to the other three principles.

The final chapter, Chapter Nine, also reflects on the journey undertaken by the project team. The journey is contextualised against both USQ and Australian higher education imperatives to draw out threads related to the rapid changes impacting on higher education, in particular technological innovation, managerial governance, and quality assurance. In so doing, the chapter reviews the applicability of the five principles in constituting the core of a pedagogical approach. The approach needs to retain its relevance and be agile enough to respond ably to rapid and complex shifts in the contemporary higher education environment. Chapter Nine thus anticipates a conceptual framework for developing a relevant, responsive, and agile institutional pedagogy.

This refereed volume provides an opportunity to gain insights about the development of pedagogy in a regional university as well as its capacity to reflect and to build staff and student knowledge, skills, and capabilities and connect them to the university's strategic plan.

—Jill Lawrence

ACKNOWLEDGEMENTS

We thank Emeritus Professor Frank Crowther, former Dean of Education at USQ, and Pro Vice-Chancellor Social Justice and Community Engagement, 2003-2006, for his leadership of the transnational project team and vision to create a transnational pedagogy.

We also acknowledge the work of the transnational project team, who provided the important groundwork for this book: Nura Behjat, Dawn Birch, Lyn Brodie, Lorelle Burton, Bryan Connors, Patricia Cretchley, Ann Dashwood, Andrew Hoey, Jill Lawrence, Alice Brown, Jason Locke, Jerry Maroulis, Alan Smith, and Dave Wood.

We are grateful to the support of our research assistants: Robert White, Kathryn Chalmers, and Dorothy Bramston and the particular contribution of Helen Hauff to Chapters Two and Three.

We appreciate the advice and critical comment from our peer reviewers who helped inform the current volume–Pat Danaher, David Dowling, Linda Galligan, Sara Hammer, Megan Kek, Marian Lewis, Noah Mbano, Jacquie McDonald, Warren Midgley, Karen Noble, Shirley O'Neill, Glen Postle, Michael Sankey, Michael Singh, Jane Summers, and Karen Trimmer.

We thank our communications editor, Andrew Fox and typesetter, Adam McAuley, for their expertise and commentary.

Funding: The research projects outlined in this volume were funded by various USQ grants, including a 2006 USQ Learning and Teaching Enhancement Committee Competitive Grant–*Transnational Pedagogies: From Principles to Practice;* and a 2009-2010 USQ Associate Teaching and Learning Fellowship–*Realising the Potential of a Self-Assessment of Learning and Teaching (SALT) tool.*

CHAPTER ONE

THE JOURNEY:
AN INSTITUTIONAL PEDAGOGY
IN THE MAKING

ANN DASHWOOD, JILL LAWRENCE,
LORELLE BURTON, AND ALICE BROWN

Introduction

In 2005, the University of Southern Queensland (USQ) announced its vision to be *Australia's leading transnational university*. With the term "transnational" open to interpretation, the incumbent Pro Vice-Chancellor (Regional Engagement and Social Justice) initiated a project team to define a transnational pedagogy for USQ. The transnational project (TP) team was drawn from across the University, comprising Excellence in Teaching Award winners and noted teachers nominated by their faculties. The team had two aims: to identify pedagogical practices that were transnational in nature; and to describe good practices in teaching and learning that exemplified "transnational pedagogy" in an Australian tertiary institution.

This chapter documents the TP team's journey in exploring uncontested knowledge and multiple perspectives to reach consensus for defining an approach to transnational teaching and learning. The goal was to produce a statement of principles to serve as the University's teaching mission. Research could then evaluate the efficacy of this framework by identifying perceptions that academics and students held about the principles. Re-examining teaching and learning this way enabled the team to reproblematise the legitimacy of dominant assumptions and evolve new paradigms. The morphing of past practice into a pedagogy which has been ecologically modified for the digital era is part of the scholarship of teaching and learning presented here.

Higher Education Perspectives

A university's managerial and administrative functions are more likely to define its leadership than the pedagogy it represents. Crowther and Burton (2007) argued that "traditional conceptions of university leadership, with their emphasis on strategic and managerial processes, are difficult to reconcile with developmental initiatives such as generation of an institutional pedagogy" (p. 11). In this process, academics function independently as in the past, without an explicit pedagogy (Crowther & Burton, 2007). Crowther and Burton (2007) asserted that a distributed leadership approach, this time through pedagogical functions, was an alternative. This approach empowers staff to own the pedagogical process. However it does have some risks, including the possibility that the vision could be wrong and that academics are directed to function on a flawed premise (Crowther & Burton, 2007).

Recent years have seen an international trend towards enhanced teaching and learning effectiveness in universities. Sorcinelli and Austin (2006, as cited in Crowther & Burton, 2007) used Senge's (1990) concept of a "learning organisation" as evidenced by faculty development in North America. The most effective institutions for the future are those "that approach educational development as collaborative, community work" (Sorenson, 2006, p. 21) and are engaged in authentic teaching (Newmann, Secada, & Wehlage, 1995). These initiatives highlighted the responsibility of higher education to contribute to the quality of community life and democratic capacity. Holland (2005) claimed that engaged scholarship with engaged teaching and learning was "to be a force for institutional change and diversity" (p. 12). Higher education had to relate to the wider world. The Australian Commonwealth Government introduced reforms aimed at enhancing university teaching, primarily through funding incentives (Rivers, 2004). Universities around Australia called for plans to convert a "real world learning" vision into authentic student experiences (Young, 2006, as cited in Crowther & Burton 2007):

> We are turning the traditional learning model around. We will be delivering a practical problem for all students to start their studies with and through which students learn all their theoretical knowledge. So you engage students – they learn by doing things rather than being told things. (p. 6)

Conceptual Framework

The TP team used a genealogical approach. Genealogy is a relatively new methodology which looks to conceptualise current problems differently from how traditional or revisionist histories have understood them (Macfarlane and Lewis 2004). Michel Foucault (1986) introduced this method, distinguishing it from traditional history by insisting on its ability to affirm all knowledge as perspective. According to Foucault, genealogy became a way to write "the history of the present"–a diagnostic tool that foregrounds the cultural practices that have constituted us as subjects (as cited in Macfarlane & Lewis, 2004, p. 55).

Genealogy inquires into the processes, procedures, and techniques which produce truth, knowledge, and beliefs (Meadmore, Hatcher, & McWilliam 2000). This method makes participants uncomfortable, so that through shared dialogue and philosophical inquiry, and by exploring concepts, values, and positions, they can become more comfortable. McWilliam (2004) suggested this methodology allows us to view problems differently, as it is neither judgemental nor problem-solving, but uses a detached evaluation and assessment through multiple perspectives.

Methodology

The genealogical approach enabled the TP team to revisit a number of their uncontested ways of knowing in relation to (a) pedagogical practices that were "transnational", and (b) criteria for good practice in teaching and learning that exemplified "transnational pedagogy" in Australia. The process questioned legitimacy of the status quo thereby allowing established paradigms and "particular truths" to be dismantled and viewed through a "new lens" (Meadmore et al., 2000, p. 465). Through this process, the team discovered new knowledge and understandings of transnational pedagogy.

The concept of "transnational pedagogy" is problematic as it has a number of different and conflicting meanings in the higher education context (see Stage 2 below). The genealogical approach allowed the TP team to test ideas and shape a shared understanding of the concept.

The TP team set out to define USQ's transnational pedagogy by operationalising the transnational agenda for local and global higher educational goals. The genealogical approach acted as a diagnostic tool to problematise the stages along the journey, using consultation and collaboration throughout. The six stages included: problematising, reflecting on past and present practices, re-evaluating truths, developing shared understandings, evolving processes, and identifying future possibilities (Tamboukou, 2003). The process of collaborating across the University and conceptualising a framework of transnational teaching and learning developed into an historical record of how learning and teaching principles have evolved with time across the USQ community.

The Project Team Participants

There were 15 members of the TP team (see Crowther et al., 2005). That many of the team were USQ Teaching Excellence Award winners reflected advancements, documented above, in learning and teaching at the national level. For example, the Carrick Institute for Learning and Teaching in Higher Education (2006) set benchmarks for university teaching quality, attributing quality to academic programs that were exemplars of the following four characteristics: (a) distinctiveness, coherence, and clarity of purpose; (b) positive influence on student learning and student engagement; (c) breadth of impact; and (d) concern for equity and diversity. In 2006 and 2007 at USQ, ten individuals and/or teams received Carrick Institute Citations for Outstanding Contributions to Student Learning while five individuals and/or teams received Carrick Awards for Australian University Teaching. Four members of the TP team were both Carrick Citation and Award winners. Qualities of transnational pedagogy are also inherent in the Carrick awardees' teaching and learning philosophies and practices. Defining transparency of good practice in local and global contexts, as recognised by the Carrick Institute, and determining the extent to which USQ embedded those characteristics in its programs, provided a focus for the transnational pedagogy journey.

The Transnational Journey

The TP team met several times throughout 2005 and 2006 for 2-hour sessions of face-to-face informal gatherings. Between meetings, electronic postings allowed the participants to review and reflect on their proposals. Ideas were proposed, shared, questioned, debated, recorded, and reviewed during the meetings. The process interconnected with the genealogical approach as it sought to inquire into the processes, procedures, and techniques which produce knowledge (Meadmore et al., 2000; Williams, 2005). The six stages of the process are outlined below.

Stage 1: Problematisation

This stage identifies and isolates the problem (Tamboukou, 1999; 2003). Knowledge assumptions of truth were subjected to inquiry and contested (Henriques, Hollway, Urwin, Venn, & Walkerdine, 1998; Hook, 2001). Tamboukou (2003) argued a kind of "socially shared 'discomfort' about how things are going" initiates this stage (p. 18). The team problematised the concept of transnational pedagogy, then set themselves the task of defining its principles and strategies for USQ.

The rationale the team accepted encompassed the ideas that:

1. The USQ vision as *Australia's leading transnational educator* explicitly promotes the concept of balancing global/regional values in all aspects of our daily work. The implications for our professional practice were deemed worth teasing out.
2. The concept of "transnational education" manifests a responsible, futuristic concern for global well-being and sustainability–something we care about very much and want to fully reflect in our work.
3. Creating a better picture of what transnational pedagogy meant would provide a practical way to communicate USQ's distinctive mandate to all members of the community, particularly our students and prospective students.
4. Heightened educational outcomes are inextricably linked to agreement about, and shared responsibility for, teaching, learning, and assessment processes.
5. Clarifying a concept like transnational pedagogy would provide a meaningful basis for shared learning and professional development across USQ.

Other universities had attempted to develop frameworks for international pedagogical processes, but few had been satisfied with the results, as far as we knew (see next section). At a time when all Australian universities were being challenged to explicate their pedagogical capabilities and practices, why would we not accept this compelling challenge? The TP team's task was thus to develop and circulate their own understanding of transnational pedagogy.

Stage 2: Reflection on Past and Present Practices

In this stage, the TP team reflected on their past and present practices. The aim was to question dominant discourses and understandings (Hook, 2001). By exploring understandings at the site (the University) where ethics (rules and expectations) or styles of living (practices) interface, current understandings (uncontested truths, centres of power) are revealed, made transparent, and deconstructed (Williams, 2005). Williams (2005) suggested that it involves:

> The drawing up of a *dispositif* showing the relationship to the 'problem' of the various phenomena constituting it; the latter should include any uncontested 'truths', all centres of power, and the bodies of any individuals involved as the site where their ethics (or style of living) interface with the world. (p. 725)

This reflective stage required reviewing the literature on the concept of "transnational", a step frequently revisited throughout the process and in fact throughout the whole journey. Initially two main strands emerged. The first was a big picture view equating transnational pedagogy with good practice and inclusive teaching. The second equated transnational with offshore teaching. Jackson (2003) articulated the first understanding, stating that many Western universities were responding to the demands of globalisation by introducing an element of multiculturalism to their curricula. Jackson isolated three main assumptions in this process: (a) globalisation is a viable agenda for a sustainable and just future for all people; (b) the university is obligated to respond faithfully to current demands of western society, in this case for globalisation; and (c) given the first two assumptions, internationalising the curriculum is a logical response. Jackson argued that we must recognise and question the first two assumptions, to challenge the foundational concepts of contemporary Western civilisation. The core concepts of other cultures may be an asset in this process, giving an entirely new meaning to the term "internationalisation of the curriculum" (Jackson, 2003). Chapter Nine will continue to explore this argument, revitalising it with the contemporary literature.

The University of South Australia (UniSA), an established transnational educator, proceeded with the assumptions put forward by Jackson (2003). At the UniSA, transnational education had become well established with Australian academics teaching students in their local contexts, face-to-face, and offshore. The meaning of transnational education at UniSA included taking courses and programs and teaching them overseas. UniSA offered courses offshore with local tutors from participating partner institutions, raising many issues for academics. For example, cultural and educational experiences of students based in Asian countries raised a wider range of expectations, however teachers had to explain to students that "the process of learning is just as important as the content" (UniSA, 2007, p. 1) and that they had to be encouraged to engage with content and process as a scholarly activity using their higher learning skills. Preparation of material, with meaningful assessment tasks, was coupled with an effort to "show empathy for your students, develop effective relationships with students, stimulate the flow of ideas, and encourage, challenge, support, listen and model" (UniSA, 2007, p. 1). It was not sufficient to replicate the textual material delivered in Australia. Elsewhere, the University of Western Australia saw its offshore programs in terms of the impact of culture on learning, considering diverse student needs and capabilities, teacher perspectives, and determining how best to design and deliver appropriate learning materials and library services (Thompson, 2003).

The second and more salient strand effectively delineated between the terms "transnational" and "pedagogy", given that strategic directions many universities were taking at that time equated transnational with offshore teaching. Monash University, for example, had in place transnational quality assurance practices with institutions and companies abroad. Shoemaker (2008) later argued that Monash had gone further down this road than any other Australian university, expanding to include campuses in South Africa and Malaysia. Swinburne University of Technology, Curtin University and the University of Wollongong also followed this path. The rationale included the provision of the institution's programs through direct contact with faculty staff and facilities, rather than surrendering the responsibility to private offshore course providers who may also offer courses approved by rival institutions. Potential students are also able to study at a much lesser cost than studying in Australia.

This reflective stage for the TP team involved reviewing the literature on the concept of "pedagogy". Pedagogy, the art and science of education, ranges from skills acquisition (Gagne, 1965) to the full development of the human being (Bernstein, 2000) to critical pedagogy (Freire, 1970). It utilises a framework under which teachers choose and develop cognitive strategies in relation to the discipline they are teaching, the quality of learning environment they develop, while taking into account the learning styles and backgrounds of their students, and the level of authentic assessment. Also involved is consideration of their own philosophy and array of teaching strategies as well as their capacity to select and apply those most appropriate (Department of Education, Training and Employment,

2004). Chapter Nine revisits this literature, considering ongoing change in contemporary education.

Stage 3: Re-Evaluation of Truths

Questioning was fundamental to this stage, prioritising questions about "where are we" and "where can we go" (Henriques et al., 1998). Williams (2005) spoke of the need to pose challenging questions with detachment and meticulous scrutiny, both textual and non-textual. This stage privileges "how" over "why" questions in the historical analysis of the "problem", and concentrates on its "conditions of possibility".

Subsequent meetings further questioned the TP team's knowledge assumptions. Questions such as "which strand of research reflects the group's evolving understandings of transnational?" were fundamental, and, if the group were to take the first view of equating transnational pedagogy with good practice, it had to consider what this meant for pedagogy at USQ. At UniSA, for example, Leask (2004) found that local staff offshore, from partner organisations, collaborated in the teaching support to visiting lecturers and the students. They usually shared the language and educational backgrounds of the students and were key mediators of the curriculum. USQ confronts similar challenges. Teachers have to manage heavy workloads and large classes, often within severe time constraints. They must also build relationships with new students and bridge the "cultural gap" with students. They must adapt content delivery for the offshore cohort and use more effective communication skills to encourage interactivity in classes. Students must boost their assertiveness and teachers must teach conventions of referencing to avoid plagiarism. Adequate resources are essential to this process.

This questioning process contributed to the TP team's understandings of transnational as exemplifying "distributed leadership". This stage achieved congruence by the team collaborating to define transnational pedagogy at USQ. Transnational was thus defined as "globally located" anywhere that USQ students were studying, either online, on-campus, or by distance education. It began with local in Toowoomba, to trans-continental within Australia reaching interstate rural and urban locations, inter-continental to Asia, North America and Europe, and trans-oceanic to the Pacific and island neighbours.

Stage 4: Development of Shared Understandings

It is important to arrive at a shared meaning that is fluid and evolving; to generate a new understanding developed from a conglomeration of shared discursive forms (Henriques et al., 1998). Henriques et al. (1998) stated that "it is then possible to put together a new proposal for the present that takes account of all the different discursive forms which went into the making of the original concept" (p. 100).

Having arrived at a shared meaning of transnational, the team set out to define "USQ pedagogy". The team concurred that "good teaching practice" represented the pedagogy and that they would need to circulate any agreed definition of "transnational pedagogy" across the University community for comment. Within the team, views were made known and supporting evidence identified. The following debate was often based on establishing priorities rather than rejections. When a concept had been sufficiently clarified, consensus was reached and it became part of that meeting's unfolding clarification of the pedagogy based on good practice among colleagues.

The learning and teaching goals the TP team identified included: showing respect for students, possessing a passion for teaching and learning, showing insight into existing skills and knowledge, clarifying student and teacher expectations, communicating effectively, actively engaging students in learning, providing a cross-cultural perspective, reflecting continuously on one's teaching, being open to change, and collaborating with colleagues. The team redeveloped the definition of "transnational" and put forward ideas on the "pedagogy" that best described good practice at USQ. They put these ideas into two categories. First, they outlined the principles of teaching practice. Second, they described the strategies for implementing enhanced learning.

Stage 5: Evolution of Processes

Hook (2001) argued that the last principle of genealogical methodology is exteriority. Thus, "that in analysis the apparent meaning of a discourse must give way before the external conditions of its possibility" (Hook, 2001, p. 538). Williams (2005) maintained that this stage is a combination of detachment and meticulous scrutiny. To disseminate the pedagogy to the broader USQ community, the TP team presented the proposed USQ transnational principles and strategies at a number of USQ forums through 2005 and 2006. The principles were also presented to an international forum and through consultation and research meetings held in 2007.

In the first stage of dissemination, the academic community met to discuss the principles. This was an initial step to obtain the University's endorsement and embed them as the basis of transnational pedagogy at USQ. The group felt that putting the principles into action required exemplars of good practice. The TP team had to provide evidence of good practice which had been formally acknowledged. As a result, the TP team put together exemplars of best practice from across their various disciplines.

The team chose the USQ common hour to communicate the principles and strategies. The forum goals were two-fold: (a) to present the concept to the USQ academic community, and (b) to communicate the journey of identifying a transnational pedagogy framework. The team defined the key concepts, with exemplars added to provide discipline-specific input. Individuals in the audience were then invited to provide input, providing personal exemplars and raising questions about the stated vision. Written comments were canvassed and the feedback collated, and then reviewed by a small subgroup. A second presentation was made to an international forum held at USQ in December 2005 by then Pro Vice-Chancellor (Regional Engagement and Social Justice), with break-out groups including team members. The concepts encapsulated an orientation to strategic teaching rather than a prescription for ways in which specific disciplines might implement each strategy.

Each public forum outlined the essential characteristics of the major principles, in order to identify teaching strategies that would give them authenticity. This helped problematise the principles and strategies of transnational pedagogy for newcomers, who were often key stakeholders (e.g., USQ policy makers). Each presentation received questioning and sometimes hostile feedback. A major issue was a perception that "transnational" meant shifting USQ's priority from local to global orientation of student needs. There was concern that the image presented should not be the definitive direction for USQ. Second, some believed that a documented statement of a "transnational pedagogy" would not be sustained in practice. This would bring USQ into contempt if it was shown that the University did not meet its marketed image.

The consultation process enabled the TP team to reshape the initial principles and strategies. The five key principles that evolved included:

1. *The Sustainability Principle:* USQ embraces the ability to meet present needs within a code of ethical practice without compromising the ability to meet future needs.

2. *The Engagement Principle*: USQ fosters engagement and collaboration. Engagement means participating in interactive exchanges of knowledge. Collaboration means working creatively in partnerships: student-to-student and teacher-to-student.
3. *The Scholarship Principle*: USQ respects diverse learning and teaching styles and upholds excellence and integrity of scholarship across disciplines.
4. *The Flexibility Principle*: USQ accepts individual and collective responsibility in providing supportive, inclusive, and flexible learning environments.
5. *The Contextual Principle*: USQ recognises and values students' backgrounds and contexts.

The team reconvened after the presentations to the wider University community to determine how to embed transnational pedagogy into future teaching protocols and practices. A position chapter was presented to University Council and was endorsed in November 2005. The Vice-Chancellor's Executive Committee unanimously endorsed it on July 6, 2006 (USQ, 2006) and it appeared in the USQ vision statement posted on the USQ homepage in 2007.

Stage 6: Identification of Future Possibilities

Williams (2005) suggested that the final stage involves identifying future possibilities and political choices as a direct result of analysing a problem, identifying and isolating new problems (Tamboukou, 2003) to be later contested (Henriques et al., 1998). For the team, this final stage meant choosing whether to continue the process. Some members ended their involvement here, although papers were presented at international conferences the following year.

The endorsement of the transnational pedagogy problematised new concerns for the remaining members.

Tamboukou's (2003, p. 18) notion of "socially shared 'discomfort' about how things are going" was re-established in relation to three key areas: dissemination, implementation, and research. They following issues were identified:

1. There was no precedent at USQ for an organisation-wide initiative based on the concept of "alignment". It was not part

of the conscious academic thinking at USQ and was contrary to some perspectives on academic freedom and autonomy.
2. There was a "risk" factor if the University vision was "wrong" (Crowther & Burton, 2007).
3. Moreover, there was the issue of whether it was mandatory to include the University's pedagogical framework as a basic ingredient of its marketing strategies (Crowther & Burton, 2007). USQ marketing investigations of the role of value-adding in the market have found that connectedness to the institution was an imperative in students' decision-making (I. Olton, personal communication, June 25 2007).
4. USQ's marketing division had historically created its own marketing strategies, including underlying values, without input from academic staff. The question of whether the transnational concept was compelling enough to drive USQ's marketing strategy remained unanswered.
5. Extensive university-wide professional development would be required to familiarise staff with the rationale for transnational pedagogy and to develop familiarity with the principles and strategies.
6. Workload issues were likely to arise when staff engaged in collaborative planning and collaborative professional learning.
7. Reward systems would need to be aligned with Carrick Institute Award processes for staff who demonstrate success in implementing the University vision through their pedagogical practices.

These issues were resolved in various ways. The challenges raised in the first three issues are discussed further in Chapter Nine. Whether a consequence of the negative feedback or more reflective of the technological shifts increasingly impacting on the higher education sector, the transnational label was superseded in 2007 with changes in USQ's institutional strategic directions, a development alleviating the concerns raised above (issue 4). Professional development and workload issues (issues 5 and 6) continue to be ongoing while the reward systems (issue 7) have been implemented.

Moving Forward: The Next Steps

The TP team disbanded in late 2006, its role having come to an end. However the Director of the Centre for Research in Transformative

Pedagogies, based in the Faculty of Education, was invited to respond to the University-endorsed statement on transnational pedagogy. The research centre was to prioritise research related to transnational pedagogy. The outcomes included a research plan to conduct funded research, collecting evidence of the community's understanding of notions surrounding transnational pedagogy related to their program.

Early in 2007, Dr Burton called a research meeting to gather individual and collective interest in the notion of surveying transnational pedagogy. One group, focused around a Faculty of Education research grant and comprising the authors of this book, developed an online survey instrument to be used in semesters two and three (2007) to gather a university wide concept from students and staff about the extent to which learning and teaching at USQ are transnational. The survey items were based on the principles outlined by the TP team. The research group developed one version of the survey for students and one for academic staff. The student survey was disseminated in September 2007 and the academic staff survey in February 2008. The results are reported in Chapters Three, Four and Five of this book. A Self-Assessment of Learning and Teaching (SALT) matrix was later developed in 2010 on the five key principles of pedagogy in the higher education sector and reviewed by academics in focus groups. Their responses are reflected in Chapters Seven and Eight, respectively.

Conclusion

The journey of the TP team in using the genealogical process to define the concept of "transnational pedagogy" was at first troubling then rewarding. Higher education practice had evolved from traditional face-to-face practice to offering courses offshore, a shift which caused the project team to rethink the shared understandings of key principles of higher education going forward. The use of the genealogical approach instigated an awareness of pedagogical practices from changing from being "transnational" in nature to embracing an evolving pedagogy for the ever changing times. This approach also extended ways of identifying good practice in teaching and learning. USQ had thus developed an educational vision to underpin its transnational mission. The stages of the journey overviewed in this chapter also involved disseminating the pedagogy to the faculties and identifying strategic directions in pedagogical practice within existing University frameworks. It also meant shaping research tools to inform practice that connects the intellectual demands of a campus-based pedagogy with the demands of distance education across digital domains.

From this point the ongoing productive pedagogy journey involved establishing the University's teaching practices around five principles. It was intended that the principles be embedded into course resources that reflected the roles of teachers, learners and materials in an era of globalisation. The team envisaged that, as the principles were put into practice, the University would become distinctive in the Australian higher education sector for the transnational pedagogy it had constructed. The future journey would be prospective, based on a process of introspection, analysis, integration, innovation, and improvement (Crowther et al., 2005). Research findings within the University and with international partners would also continue to inform the transnational pedagogy genre. It was also hoped that a pilot study of USQ students and academics would provide the catalyst for assessing the framework. A key question would be to determine how teachers recognised in their practices the principles of transnational teaching and learning and to understand the extent to which students perceived the pedagogy benefited their learning. Chapter Two describes the theoretical perspectives underlying the concepts developed by the TP team. The chapter explains how a newer and smaller research team (consisting of the four authors of this book) reviewed the five principles to explore how they were perceived in USQ's learning and teaching work.

References

Bernstein, B. (2000). *Pedagogy, symbolic control and identity: Theory, research, critique* (Rev. ed.). London: Rowman & Littlefield.

Carrick Institute for Learning and Teaching in Higher Education. (2006). *Carrick awards for Australian university teaching: Awards for programs that enhance learning: Promoting and advancing learning and teaching in Australian higher education.* Retrieved August 30, 2007, from http://www.carrickinstitute.edu.au/carrick/go/home/awards/pid/60

Crowther, F., Behjat, N., Birch, D., Brodie, L., Burton, L., Connors, B., Cretchley, P., Dashwood, A., Hoey, A., Lawrence, J., Brown, A., Locke, J., Maroulis, J., Smith, A. and Wood, D. (2005). *Transnational pedagogy: A stimulus paper for consideration by the USQ professional community.* Unpublished manuscript, University of Southern Queensland, Toowoomba, Australia.

Crowther, F., & Burton, L. (2007). *Aligning organisational vision and academic practices: Implications for University strategic planners.* A keynote presentation at the Knowledge Partnerships Conference on Higher Education: International Markets, Internal Dynamics, Cambridge, United Kingdom.

Department of Education, Training and Employment. (2004). *Productive pedagogies.* Retrieved from the State of Queensland Department of Education, Training and Employment website: http://education.qld.gov.au/corporate/newbasics/html/pedagogies/peda gog.html

Foucault, M. (1986). Nietzsche, genealogy and history. In P. Rabinow (Ed.), *The Foucault reader* (pp. 101-120). London: Penguin.

Freire, P. (1970). *Pedagogy of the oppressed.* New York: Continuum.

Gagne, R. M. (1965). *The condition of learning* (1st ed.). New York: Holt, Reinhart and Winston.

Henriques, J., Hollway, W., Urwin, C., Venn, G., & Walkerdine, V. (1998). *Changing the subject: Psychology, social regulation and subjectivity.* London: Routledge.

Holland, B. A. (2005). Scholarship and mission in the 21st century university: The role of engagement. *AUQA Occasional Publication Proceedings of the Australian Universities Quality Forum 2005,* p. 12. Retrieved from http://depts.washington.edu/ccph/pdf_files/AUQA_paper_final_05.pdf

Hook, D. (2001). Discourse, knowledge, materiality, history: Foucault and discourse analysis. *Theory and Psychology, 11*(4).

Jackson, M. G. (2003) Internationalising the university curriculum. *Journal of Geography in Higher Education,* 27 (3), 325 – 340. Retreived 22 May 2008, http://www.informaworld.com/smpp/content~content=a715702473~db =all

Leask, B. (2004, July). *Transnational education and intercultural learning: Reconstructing the offshore teaching team to enhance internationalisation.* Paper presented at the Australian Universities Quality Forum: Quality in a Time of Change, Adelaide, South Australia.

Macfarlane, K., & Lewis, T. (2004). Childcare: Human services or education: A genealogical approach. *Contemporary Issues in Early Childhood, 5*(1), 51-67.

McWilliam, E. (2004). W(h)ither practitioner research? *The Australian Educational Researcher, 31*(2), 113-126.

Meadmore, D., Hatcher, C., & McWilliam, E. (2000). Getting tense about genealogy. *International Journal of Qualitative Studies in Education, 13*(5), 463-476.

Newmann, F. M., Secada, W. G., & Wehlage, G. G. (1995). *A guide to authentic instruction and assessment: Vision, standards, and scoring.* Madison, WI: Wisconsin Center for Educational Research.

Rivers, J. (2004, April 6). Quality teaching comes under spotlight. *Campus Review*, p. 5.

Senge, P. (1990). *The fifth discipline: The art and practice of the learning organisation.* New York: Doubleday/Currency.

Shoemaker, A. (2008). *If the world is our campus, where are we going?* Retrieved from http://www.monash.edu.au/teaching/passport/paper.html

Sorenson, L. (2006, April). Educational development in the USA. *HERDSA News*, pp. 19-21.

Tamboukou, M. (1999). Writing genealogies: An exploration of Foucault's strategies for doing research. *Discourse: Studies in the Cultural Politics of Education, 29*(2), 201-217.

—. (2003). *Women, education and the self: A Foucauldian perspective.* Basingstoke, UK: Palgrave.

Thompson, E. (2003). New partners in learning: An effective teaching and learning framework for offshore students. Proceedings of the 12th Annual Teaching Learning Forum, 11-12 February 2003. Perth: Edith Cowan University. Retrieved from: http://lsn.curtin.edu.au/tlf/tlf2003/abstracts/thompsonabs.html

University of South Australia. (2007). *Transnational teaching: An overview.* Retrieved from http://www.unisanet.unisa.edu.au/learningconnection/staff/practice/transnational-overview.asp

University of Southern Queensland. (2006). *USQ equity update 2006.* Retrieved June 4, 2007, from the University of Southern Queensland website: http://www.usq.edu.au/planstats/planning/docs/USQEquityUpdate2006.doc

Williams, A. (2005). Genealogy as methodology in the philosophy of Michel Foucault. *London Foucault Circle* Retrieved from http://www.uel.ac.uk/cnr/documents/GenealogyasMethodologyinthePhilosophyofMichelFoucault_001.doc

Young, I. (2006, July 19). Swinburne rewrites its curricula. *Campus Review*, p. 5.

CHAPTER TWO

REVIEWING FIVE KEY PRINCIPLES OF PEDAGOGY

LORELLE BURTON, JILL LAWRENCE, ANN DASHWOOD, AND ALICE BROWN,

Introduction

As documented in Chapter One, the transnational project (TP) team developed a transnational pedagogy at the University of Southern Queensland (USQ) encompassing five key learning and teaching principles: Sustainability, Engagement, Scholarship, Flexibility, and Contextual Learning. In 2005, the consultative project team identified learning and teaching practices that were transnational in nature and reflective of good practice. Over a period of months, the team engaged in reflective and action-based research to investigate "transnationality" in their teaching and learning practices (Crowther et al., 2005). Outcomes from these activities were discussed and debated at regular meetings, culminating in the creation of a rationale for "transnational pedagogy" and the development of the five associated pedagogical principles. The next step involved identifying the theoretical framework underpinning these five key principles.

This chapter provides a theoretical review of the concepts embedded in each of the five principles. The review examines the understandings that the TP team had attributed to the principles. The chapter also explores how these theoretical perspectives informed the research team in developing an online survey to measure student and staff perceptions of the five learning and teaching principles and how they relate to practice at USQ. The longitudinal nature of our journey means the current chapter also documents our initial literature review of the principles. Chapters Seven, Eight, and Nine further revitalise this literature to accommodate the impact of change forces in contemporary Australian higher education.

Sustainability in Higher Education

The TP team understood that the Sustainability principle meant that USQ embraced the ability to meet present needs within a code of ethical practice without compromising the ability to meet future needs (Crowther et al., 2005).

Sustainability has been a relatively recent participant in higher education. In 1978, the United National Educational Scientific and Cultural Organisation (UNESCO) conference in Tbilisi prescribed the concept of environmental education, where the emphasis was an understanding of various impacts on the biophysical environment (Day and & Monroe, 2000, as cited in Thomas, 2009). Although earlier environmental education focused on developing knowledge about the environment, after the Tbilisi conference, education associated with the environment emerged as a new focal point, introducing the element of values favouring the environment. The idea of "sustainable development" was broached in the Brundtland Report of the World Commission on Environment and Development (Brundtland, 1987, as cited in Thomas, 2009, p. 246) arguing that human behaviour was threatening the world's ability "to meet the needs of the present generation without compromising the ability of future generations to meet their own needs". Thomas (2009) described the evolution of sustainability in the education context since then:

> In the 1980s, the political undertones of including environmental values in curriculum had the potential to be a liberating concept that transformed the thinking of both teachers and students. Subsequently, the addition of social and economic considerations to those of the environment expanded the concepts of this educational field, but the tendency has still been to focus on knowledge. More recent developments have moved the focus onto education for sustainability, with its promotion of understanding the need for supporting sustainable lifestyles. (p. 246)

Consequently, since the early 1990s, there have been many calls for universities to offer education for sustainable development as one way of minimising the disconnection between humans and the natural environment (Thomas, 2009). Australian and European universities have responded by initiating research into sustainable learning and teaching (Kennedy, 2006). Filho (2000) observed that sustainability had multiple uses within the higher education sector. During the first decade of the 21st century, for example, universities committed themselves to the sustainability concept through various declarations and charters (e.g., the Halifax Declaration, the Bologna Charter, the 2010 Campus Sustainability

Review, and the Australasian Campuses towards Sustainability Network; Kennedy, 2006). The UNESCO World Conference on Education for Sustainable Development encompassed broad parameters in its declaration:

> ...setting a new direction for education and learning for all. It promotes quality education, and is inclusive of all people... it is based on values, principles, and practices necessary to respond effectively to current and future challenges. (Bonn Declaration 2009, p. 1)

Despite these initiatives, an agreed interpretation of sustainability remained elusive (Kennedy, 2006). Several research strands emerged facilitating this impression. One strand encompassed its interdisciplinary nature, relating sustainability across diverse discipline areas (Thomas, 2009). This strand linked sustainability with critical thinking and problem solving. For example, sustainability emphasises creative and critical approaches, long-term thinking, innovation, and empowerment for dealing with uncertainty, and solving complex problems (Thomas, 2009). The term also expanded into transformative learning (Moore, 2005).

Other discussions about sustainability were linked to lifelong learning, cultural and contextual considerations and ethics. For example, Jashke (2007) believed "sustainability" should be (a) specific to context, (b) evolving, and (c) an open-ended process. She further argued that it may be "more helpful to seek to set out the principles and criteria that ought to govern such processes than to aim at text-book definitions" (p. 1). Jashke proposed that sustainable education should involve a value-driven approach to teaching, that sustainability was an ethical as much as a "practical-technical" challenge and that it should operate within a comprehensive framework taking a stakeholder-orientated approach with cultural and material lifecycle considerations.

A further strand links sustainability with ethics. This strand stems from the 1987 Brundtland Report (as cited in Thomas, 2009). The original intent behind the definition of "sustainable development" allowed the co-existence of fundamental conflict between ecological systems and human cultures, indicating it was possible for humans to co-exist with natural assemblages of organisms, but a definition was required. As a result, an understanding of what was "right" and what was demonstrably "wrong" with respect to policy, technology and economic instruments were brought to bear on the environment. Though the initial clarity has been muddied substantially in the intervening years, the TP team was well placed to reclaim the primacy of the concept of "sustainability" in guiding development, and to do so in ways that are informed by highly-developed and tested science. Johnston, Everard, Santillo, and Robert (2007) maintained that:

> It is therefore important that we accept a set of higher ethical standards in order to give substance to a vision of sustainability. To do this, it will be necessary to define ethics of sustainability which can be used as a metric of achievement and success in all areas of activity. This ethical framework needs, as a priority, to address the central issue of consequences in a world of total freedoms which yet remains, wilfully or otherwise, ignorant of these consequences. (p. 63)

Another strand equated sustainability with technological developments. A Carrick Institute sponsored project (Gosper et al., 2008) was conducted at four Australian universities: Macquarie University, Murdoch University, Flinders University, and the University of Newcastle. Student and teacher surveys were used to explore understandings of how web-based practices were impacting on learning and teaching. Results indicated that there was a clear mismatch between staff and student expectations. More students (67%) than teachers (30%) believed that technological practices led to the achievement of better (more sustainable) results, and made it easier to learn (80% of students compared with 49% of teachers). Gosper et al. (2008) concluded that teachers need to experiment with new technologies and techniques for their teaching to be "more effective and sustainable in the longer term" (p. 11).

This review supports the efficacy of the TP team's initial thinking about the Sustainability principle. The team's definition accommodates Brundtland's 1987 (as cited in Thomas, 2009) view of meeting present needs without compromising the ability to meet future needs and includes the ethical focus evident in the literature. Further, the research team believe that the interdisciplinary, transformational, and technological foci described in the literature could be accommodated in the student and staff surveys. For example, the survey questions were contextualised to the discipline, philosophy, and teaching approach of the individual respondents (see Chapters Three and Six).

Engagement in Higher Education

The TP team proposed that USQ fosters engagement and collaboration. According to the team, the Engagement principle involved participating in interactive exchanges of knowledge while collaboration meant working creatively in partnerships: student-to-student and teacher-to-student (Crowther et al., 2005).

A broad range of research strands support the critical role played by student engagement in higher education. In 1995 McInnis published the first of a series of reports linking engagement with progression and retention (Krause, Hartley, James, & McInnes, 2005; McInnis, 2003). Linked to student engagement are research explored phenomena such as "disengagement" (Kuh, 2007; Marklein, 2005) and "negotiated engagement" (McInnis 2003) and another strand linked student engagement with transition (Kift, 2009; Kuh, 2007; McInnis, 2003; Tinto, 2005; Yorke, 2000; Zepke, Leach, & Prebble, 2003). Student engagement research is vital because it has been found that the more time and energy students apply to their studies, the more likely they are to develop the habits and practices needed to succeed at university (Kuh, 2005).

National projects have highlighted engagement practices. The Australasian Survey of Student Engagement (AUSSE; Coates, 2007) managed by the Australian Council for Educational Research (ACER) on behalf of participating universities in Australia and New Zealand, took place for the first time in 2007 with 25 universities. It built on foundations laid by the United States version, the National Survey of Student Engagement (NSSE, 2000). The AUSSE defined student engagement as "students' involvement with activities and conditions likely to generate high-quality learning" (ACER, 2008). It included a wide range of academic and non-academic interactions that students have. A key assumption held that learning is influenced by the way individuals participate in educationally purposeful activities. While students construct their own knowledge, learning depends on institutions and staff generating conditions that stimulate their involvement (Coates, 2007).

The research literature on engagement demonstrates that student success involves both institutional, pedagogical, and student responsibilities (McInnis, 2003). The institutional role refers to the actions and responsibilities in policies, processes, and support structures designed to engage students. It includes institutionally-led, strategic, and research-informed policies designed to enhance student engagement, including initiatives targeted at leading and transforming university culture. Kuh (2007) argued that students are more likely to engage in activities emphasised by their institution. However, institutional efforts to engage students become more complicated as the cultural and linguistic diversity of the student body increases (Krause, 2005). Some students are not only unfamiliar with the tertiary environment but they also have belief systems and cultural practices which are inconsistent with mainstream university practices (Lawrence, 2005). For example, referencing and research literacies are understood differently in different cultures, potentially leading to claims of plagiarism and collusion. Such diversity not only challenges institutional practice, it also makes more transparent the crucial nature of interrelationships between students' various kinds of "capital" (Bourdieu, 1999) and the consequences for engagement (Kantanis, 2002). Research findings have argued that institutions improve their levels of student engagement by adapting their cultures to meet student learning needs (see Burton & Dowling, 2005; Nelson & Kift, 2005).

Another focus in the literature centres on student responsibilities, the strategies and behaviours they need to demonstrate their engagement in learning. Hu and Kuh (2002) have argued that engagement includes behaviours such as coming to class prepared, interacting with learning materials outside of class, and using the available support services. Others have recognised that effort and peer support represent facets of engagement (Benn, 2000). Kuh (2003) asserted that the most important determinants of student success relate to the amount of time and effort students put into their studies and university life, while studying with other students adds considerable value.

While such literature highlights the role of students' self efficacy, it does not advance specific and concrete capabilities they can use to engage actively with their studies. To offset the lack of specific strategies, Lawrence (2005) developed "skills of engagement" identified as three practices:

1. Reflective practice which emphasises students' capacities to observe, to watch, and to listen to the socio-cultural practices occurring in the context.
2. Socio-cultural practice in which newcomers establish interpersonal relations and communicate effectively with mainstream hosts to reap maximum benefits from an unfamiliar context. This practice stems from cross-cultural communication theory (Bandura, 1986; Hofstede, 1997).
3. Critical practice, which encompasses twin capacities of critical self awareness and awareness of power configurations. First, students develop critical self-awareness of their own belief systems and cultural practices and second, students become critically aware of the power configurations of discourse impacting on them and the context in which they find themselves.

These three practices were later found to enhance student engagement significantly in courses and university life (Lawrence, 2007).

The literature on engagement continues to grow as researchers grapple with the dynamics of online engagement. Coates (2005) linked student engagement to quality assurance determinations. Coates argued for the need to take account of how and to what extent students engage with activities that are likely to lead to productive learning. Herrington, Oliver, and Reeves (2003) examined the role of student engagement within course units as constructivist philosophy and considered how advances in technology impact on educational design and practice. They argued that support for students in the early weeks of immersion in student-centred learning environments was critical. This was particularly important "in Online learning environments where isolation can be an additional mitigating factor against successful engagement with the course", and aligns with Taplin's (2000) contention that "acceptance of problem based learning scenarios, in addition to the usual difficulties in conventional situations, is exacerbated by distance because of the students' physical isolation" (Herrington et al.. 2003,p. 286) .

The TP team enunciated the Engagement principle as fostering collaboration between teachers and learners through participation in interactive exchanges of knowledge and that collaboration meant working creatively in partnerships, student-to-student, and teacher-to-student (Crowther et al., 2005). The literature review reinforces the TP team's definition of the Engagement principle, verifying its effectiveness as a unifying principle, whose presence in learning and teaching practices at USQ is worthy of further investigation.

Scholarship in Higher Education

The TP team defined the Scholarship principle as USQ respecting diverse learning and teaching styles and upholding excellence and integrity of scholarship across disciplines (Crowther et al., 2005).

The literature reveals many features of scholarship. One aspect that Boyer (1990) articulated in "Scholarship Reconsidered" relates to an academic's increased awareness of how to foster meaning-making among learners. He identified four areas of academic work: discovery; integration by making connections across the disciplines, placing specialities in a larger context; application; and teaching. Scholarship in pedagogy includes knowledge about teaching and learning underpinned by the subject discipline and interdisciplinary awareness and relevance to the subject of study. Shulman (2004) maintained that "teaching and consequent student learning are both worthy of scholarly inquiry and absolutely necessary if teachers are to fulfil their professional responsibility to their students" (p. 1). As a form of reflective inquiry, scholarship requires users of the tools to probe more deeply into aspects of their practice by using templates that provide conceptual frameworks and which prompt questioning.

In a global sense, the scholarship of teaching involves academics engaging with research into teaching and learning. Critical reflection (Ramsden, 2003; Robson, 2006) on professional practice requires in-depth communication within discipline-specific contexts (Healey, 2000). In Australia, Trigwell, Martin, Benjamin, and Prosser (2000) rated scholarly teaching and learning as the core business of all our universities. A scholarly teaching perspective is discipline-specific, reflective, inquisitorial, responsive, and communicative (Trigwell et al., 2000). The discipline in practice is reflected in the learning activities set for students. Discipline-based activity is reflected in curriculum documentation, in classroom materials and resources, and through writings that contribute to the discipline.

However, scholarly practice is not exclusively intra-disciplinary. It can also be oriented across disciplines, focusing on the underlying processes of learning and teaching. The multi-faceted nature of scholarship anticipates the role of communication. Scholars live life as members of active communities engaged in conversation and evaluation in which scholarship is "community property...shared, discussed, critiqued, exchanged, built on" (Shulman, 1993, p. 6). In practice, teachers focus on teaching and learning, the student experience, and learning outcomes. They use a range of mechanisms to monitor, record, and reflect on student learning. The teacher enquires into prior student learning and current expectations, and uses several monitoring mechanisms to evaluate the student learning experience and achievement of learning outcomes.

At USQ, the practice of scholarship aligns with teaching and research as an essential academic function. The University's mission, values, and vision statements underpin its policy on research and scholarship. "Scholarship refers to the analysis and interpretation of existing knowledge aimed at improving, through publications, teaching or by other means of communication, the depth of human understanding" (USQ, 2008a, part 7). Both this view and the current literature review support the TP team's initial definition of the Scholarship principle in relation to respecting diverse learning and teaching styles and upholding excellence and integrity of scholarship across USQ disciplines (Crowther et al., 2005). Subsequent chapters (Chapters Three, Six, and Seven) will explore its presence in learning and teaching practices at USQ. Chapter Nine will examine more broadly the relevance of the Scholarship principle to current practice in higher education.

The Scholarship principle interacts with the other key principles, providing the grounds for learning and teaching to be informed and contested, and supported by evidence in the light of contemporary research. Scholarship is thus intrinsic to an institution's learning and teaching pedagogy and is worthy of further investigation.

Flexibility in Higher Education

The TP team argued that the Flexibility principle required both individual and collective responsibility across USQ in creating supportive, inclusive, and flexible learning environments (Crowther et al., 2005).

The literature, along with rapid technological change, confirms the continuing relevance of flexibility in Australian higher education. In 2000, the Australian Government issued the following challenge to the Australian higher education community (Commonwealth of Australia, 2000): "Given the flexibility and means to do so, universities will be the fundamental drivers for the Australian information economy" (p. 1). This challenge remains a top priority for the Australian government, as illustrated in a recent announcement by Prime Minister Julia Gillard, then Minister for Education, Employment and Workplace Relations. During her 10 November speech at the 2008 Curriculum Corporation Conference, Gillard stated that "flexible curriculum" was highly important and that Australian education institutions will "need a rigorous curriculum with the right level of flexibility" to achieve an education system exemplifying "excellence and equity, productivity and participation" (Commonwealth of Australia, 2008b, p. 1).

In response to this challenge, many Australian higher education institutions have moved to provide flexible learning, teaching, and delivery. Educational research focussing on appropriate learning models for the 21st century has led this change. It has promoted student-centred flexible learning, authentic learning experiences, flexible learning spaces, and the flexible delivery of study materials as educational best practice. Flexible learning environments have also generated better knowledge transmission within universities and better knowledge transfer into the workplace and community (Commonwealth of Australia, 2008a; Jamieson & Dane, 2005, as cited in McLaughlin & Mills, 2008; Jones, Ladyshewsky, Oliver, Flavell, & Geoghegan, 2008).

The literature is supported by USQ's prioritisation of flexibility. For example, USQ currently employs the term "fleximode" to describe its flexible learning, teaching, and delivery practices. This model provides the basis for students to develop as independent lifelong learners, promotes interaction between teaching, scholarship, and research, and offers an international, culturally-sensitive curriculum with clear academic expectations and standards for both staff and students. It provides a flexible and responsive environment with choice of educational delivery modes, incorporates a range of teaching and learning strategies to accommodate students' diverse needs, and provides diverse educational experiences. Flexibility also applies to other University processes affecting students' learning, such as admissions, equity issues, and faculty organisation (USQ, 2008c). Providing students with these choices also ideally builds independent life-long learning capabilities.

Flexible learning, teaching, and delivery has underpinned the USQ learning and teaching policy since it established itself as one of Australia's leading distance-education providers in the late 20th century (USQ, 2008a). USQ defined flexibility as:

> All students have the right to receive a comparable learning experience regardless of their mode of study, location, gender, race or ethnicity. In practice, flexible learning offers students choices in what to learn, how to learn, how their learning is assessed and where and when the learning occurs. (USQ, 2008b)

The review of the Flexibility principle not only establishes its credentials as a key pedagogical principle, it also demonstrates its capacity to intersect with the other principles to re-affirm its relevance in a unifying pedagogy. The literature indicates that both staff and students need to be flexible in relation to the context and have to be flexible enough to engage students where they are. Flexibility facilitates sustainability as it ensures that the most appropriate mode, for example, is chosen to fit the purpose of the teaching strategy and is able to be sustained into the future. Thus, the Flexibility principle is integral to learning and teaching pedagogy and is worthy of research exploring its presence in learning and teaching practices at USQ.

Contextual Learning in Higher Education

In formulating the Contextual Learning principle, the TP team established that USQ recognises and values students' backgrounds and contexts (Crowther et al., 2005).

The TP team found the concepts underlying the Contextual Learning principle problematic to define. Unlike Engagement, Scholarship and

Flexibility, Context Learning does not have an established range of perspectives explicitly supporting its efficacy as a pedagogical principle. However, context is integral in a definition of pedagogy as one of its three operational components: teacher, student, and context. There are also a number of foci both in the literature and in the higher education sector reinforcing its significance.

In terms of the literature, context underpins the valuing of social justice and equity that encompasses student diversity. This includes valuing students' backgrounds and life experiences to ensure meaningful learning opportunities for all students, across borders, boundaries, and cultures (Freire, 1970). Contextualised learning and teaching requires appropriate professional development in order to best support diverse student groups to achieve their learning goals and optimise their learning journey (Leask, 2004). Contextualisation is not "internationalisation" as it calls for fundamental changes to take place to study materials, university protocols and expectations for engagement. The overall student experience should celebrate student diversity and provide effective learning and teaching opportunities (Brown & Reushle, 2009; Commonwealth of Australia, 2009; Jones et al., 2008; Krizek, Birnbaum, & Levinson, 2004; Zepke et al., 2003). Contextualised learning and teaching appreciates the backgrounds, knowledge and richness of diverse student cohorts. It acknowledges the importance of two-way communication, co-creation of understandings, collective engagement, and collaboration between student-and-student and student-and-educator in the learning journey (Elson-Green, 2007). It calls on educators to support students by tapping into resources that maximise their potential for growth and contribution. In essence, the Contextual Learning principle affirms more than just the importance of acknowledging culture or diversity in learning and teaching practices. It also emphasises the importance of recognising and celebrating students' backgrounds, values, experiences, and past learning journeys.

Context is therefore important not only in developing courses and teaching, but also in better understanding the cultural, political, sociological, and philosophical perspectives of the student and educator (Brown & Reushle, 2009; Krizek et al., 2004). Contextualised learning acknowledges the strengths, knowledge, and richness that multiple contexts and perspectives bring to a learning environment. It appreciates the complexity of global knowledge and promotes the positive exchange of practices and beliefs, and celebrates an open and inclusive community of learners (Han & Singh, 2007).

As outlined in subsequent chapters, the difficulty in defining context emanates from the relatively limited literature explicitly delineating the dimensions of context to learning and teaching. Yet context is underpinned by a host of alternate research areas. As Chapter Nine explains, these stem from student-centred learning, diversity, social learning theory, and critical theories. Another part of the difficulty lies in a corollary to the first. That context is inherent in the definition of pedagogy. Freire's (1970) approach to teaching people, for example, included teaching strategies, the instructor's own philosophical beliefs of instruction, as well as learning goals set by the student and teacher. These were governed by the pupil's background knowledge and experience, situation, and environment, or in other words, the context.

The Contextual Learning principle intersects with the other key principles. Sustainability first became relevant in specific contexts, invariably environmental. "Engaging" learning activities should also be appropriate to context. Scholarship always occurs in a context, for example, problem-based learning (PBL), active learning, learning within disciplines, or from an interdisciplinary perspective. Likewise, Flexibility is contextually constrained. For example, USQ's definition of flexible learning (USQ, 2008b) offers students choices in what to learn, how to learn, how their learning is assessed, and where and when the learning occurs, in other words, relative to their particular context.

The globalisation of higher education and the growing flexible enrolment patterns mean that students are enrolling from various contexts locally, nationally, and internationally. Contextualisation in higher education is therefore concerned with the diverse set of circumstances that impact on an individual, a group, a situation, or event, and gives meaning to its interpretation (Oers, 1997). Thus, contextual pedagogy can help give meaning to learning and relevance to its application (Brown & Reushle, 2009) by acknowledging the circumstances in which learning takes place (Vosniadou, 1991) and appreciating the diverse life experiences of students.

In sum, the literature reinforces the TP team's definition of Contextual Learning as a key pedagogical principle, with its presence in learning and teaching practices at USQ worthy of further investigation. The review demonstrates the Contextual Learning principle's capacity to intersect with the other principles to re-affirm its relevance in a unifying pedagogy.

Conclusion

The TP team developed a transnational pedagogy incorporating the five key principles of Sustainability, Engagement, Scholarship, Flexibility and Contextual Learning. Sustainability was defined as the ability to present needs within a code of ethical practice without compromising the ability to meet future needs. Engagement fosters collaboration between teachers and learners through participation in interactive exchanges of knowledge and collaboration, which encompasses working creatively in partnerships, student-to-student, and teacher-to-student. Scholarship recognises the capacity to respect diverse learning and teaching styles and uphold excellence and integrity of scholarship across disciplines. Flexibility generates supportive, inclusive, and flexible learning environments while Contextual Learning acknowledges the complexity of the student experience and values students' backgrounds.

The research literature on learning and teaching practice in relation to the five principles varied in both scope and extent. While literature on Sustainability is in its early stages, research on Engagement is substantial and well-advanced. Understandings about Scholarship are also well established and the literature on Flexibility is growing exponentially in response to the change forces foreshadowed in the preface. The Contextual Learning principle, however, is more problematic as it has not yet been explicitly articulated in the theoretical perspectives related to learning and teaching. However, its relevance to pedagogy is clearly reinforced by its integration in the very definition of pedagogy.

The current literature review supports the TP team's delineation of the principles as well as the understandings attributed to them. There were, however, some anomalies. These related to the inclusion of learning styles and approaches in Scholarship. Though it was decided to retain the explanations for each principle reached by the TP team, these anomalies will be investigated in subsequent Chapters.

Each of the principles was initially selected to underpin USQ's transnational approach to teaching, learning, and assessment. They comprised a pedagogy designed to prepare USQ students to engage as citizens, scholars, and knowledge-workers in local, national, and global contexts. Almost as soon as the transnational principles were endorsed by the USQ Academic Board, however, USQ's strategic plan again evolved. The renewed focus was on two main themes: open and flexible education; and sustainability. The USQ strategic plan 2009-2013 emphasised sustainable futures for communities and regions locally, nationally, and globally and a commitment to digital futures (USQ, 2009). In terms of learning and teaching, the aim was to provide flexible and inclusive learning experiences underpinned by a sustainable framework of quality assurance. Two of the principles had explicit roles in the new strategic plan: Flexibility and Sustainability. The other three principles, meanwhile, were also present though in less conspicuous ways. For instance, Scholarship, Context, and Engagement underpinned various University priority objectives (USQ, 2009, pp. 7-12): "USQ's most valuable resource is its staff and policies and practices must support, nurture and develop staff in the vital roles that they play across the organisation... USQ to develop ever improving strategies for optimising success for its increasingly diverse student constituency... To create fulfilling learning experiences that are focused on student objectives."

The strategic change also meant that the title of the survey, previously known as the *Transnational Survey,* morphed into the *Best Practice Learning and Teaching Survey,* given that at the time "best practice in learning and teaching" was the current theme of pedagogy and commonly used in higher education (Biggs, 2003; Dabner & Davis, 2009; Ramsden, 2003). University documents contain various references to supporting best practice in learning and teaching and the Australian Learning and Teaching Council's (ALTC) awards and citations program also refers to "best practice".

The literature review thus strengthens the argument that the five principles can together have the potential to constitute a potentially strong unifying pedagogical approach. The review confirms that the presence of the principles in learning and teaching practices at USQ are worthy of investigation, whether labelled as "transnational" or "best practice". Chapters Three, Four, Five and Six will describe the findings of student and staff surveys conducted in 2007. Chapter Nine will revisit the principles to determine if they remain relevant to the strategic change, as well as more recent USQ strategic planning. Chapter Nine will also investigate whether the principles reviewed here are agile, robust, and responsive enough to deal with the escalating change forces that continue to impact on the higher education sector.

References

Australian Council for Educational Research. (2008). *Australasian survey of student engagement. Australasia University executive summary report.* Retrieved from ACER website: http://www.acer.edu.au/auss

Bandura, A. (1986). *Social foundations of thought and action: A social cognitive theory.* Englewood Cliffs, NJ: Prentice Hall.

Benn, R. (2000). *Exploring widening participation in higher education: Targeting, retention and 'really useful knowledge'.* Seminar Presentation, USQ, Toowoomba, 15 March, 2000.

Biggs, J., (2003). Teaching for quality learning at university: what the student does. 2nd edn, Berkshire: SRHE & Open University Press.

Bonn Declaration. (2009). UNESCO World Conference on Education for Sustainable Development, 31 March -2 April, Bonn, Germany, pp.1-6. Retrieved November 28, 2012, from http://www.esd-world-conference-2009.org/fileadmin/download/ESD2009_BonnDeclaration 080409.pdf

Boyer, E. L. (1990). *Scholarship reconsidered: Priorities of the professoriate.* Princeton, NJ: The Carnegie Foundation for the Advancement of Teaching.

Bourdieu, P. (1999). *The weight of the world: Social suffering in contemporary society.* Cambridge: Polity Press.

Brown, A., & Reushle, S. (2009). *The power of connection: Sharing epistemological approaches to reach beyond knowledge and skill acquisition in an Australian higher education context.* Paper presented at the 2nd International Problem Based Learning Symposium, Singapore, Republic Polytechnic, Singapore.

Burton, L. J., & Dowling, D. G. (2005). In search of the key factors that influence student success at university. In A. Brew & C. Asmar (Eds.), *Higher education in a changing world. Research and development in higher education: Vol. 28. Proceedings of the 2005 Higher Education Research and Development Society of Australasia annual conference* (pp. 68-78). Sydney, Australia: University of Sydney.

Coates, H. (2005).The value of student engagement for higher education quality assurance. *Quality in Higher Education,* 11(1). Retrieved from http://www.tandfonline.com/doi/abs/10.1080/13538320500074915

Coates, H. (2007). Engaging learners in higher and vocational education. *Research Developments, 18*(4). Retrieved from http://research.acer.edu.au/resdev/vol18/iss18/4

Commonwealth of Australia. (2000). *The way forward - higher education action plan for the information economy: The challenge.* Retrieved from
http://www.dest.gov.au/sectors/school_education/publications_resourc es/summaries_brochures/learning_for_the_knowledge_society.htm#Th e_Way_Forward_-_Higher_Education_Action_Plan_for_the_Information_Economy

—. (2008a). *Review of Australian higher education.* Discussion Chapter, June 2008, retrieved from Department of Education, Science and Training website:
http://www.dest.gov.au/sectors/higher_education/policy_issues_review s/reviews/highered_review/default.htm#Review_of_Australian_Higher _Education_Discussion_Chapter_June_2008

—. (2008b). *Speech: 2008 curriculum corporation conference* by The Hon Julia Gillard MP Minister for Education; Minister for Employment and Workplace Relations; Minister for Social Inclusion; Deputy Prime Minister. Retrieved from http://mediacentre.dewr.gov.au/mediacentre/AllReleases/2008/November/2008CurriculumCorporationConference.htm

—. (2009). *Transforming Australia's higher education system*. Retrieved from: http://www.innovation.gov.au/HigherEducation/Documents/TransformingAusHigherED.pdfhttp://www.innovation.gov.au/HigherEducation/Documents/TransformingAusHigherED.pdf

Crowther, F., Behjat, N., Birch, D., Brodie, L., Burton, L., Connors, B., Cretchley, P., Dashwood, A., Hoey, A., Lawrence, J., Brown, A., Locke, J., Maroulis, J., Smith, A., & Wood, D. (2005). *Transnational pedagogy: A stimulus paper for consideration by the USQ professional community*. Unpublished manuscript, University of Southern Queensland, Toowoomba, Australia.

Dabner, N., & Davis, N. (2009). Developing best practices in online teaching and learning to impact students and their organisations. Paper presented at *ASCILITE 2009 Conference*. Retrieved September 1, 2010, from http://www.ascilite.org.au/conferences/auckland09/procs/dabner-poster.pdf

Filho, W. (2000). Dealing with misconceptions on the concept of sustainability. *International Journal of Sustainability in Higher Education,* 1(1), 9-19.

Elson-Green, J. (2007). Looking beyond the western perspective. *Campus Review,* p. 7.

Freire, P. (1970). *Pedagogy of the Oppressed*. New York: Continuum.

Gosper, M., Green D., McNeill, M., Phillips, R., Preston, G., &Woo, K. (2008). *The impact of web-based lecture technologies on current and future practice in learning and teaching*. Australian Learning and Teaching Council, an initiative of the Australian Government Department of Education, Employment and Workplace Relations. Retrieved from http://www.cpd.mq.edu.au/teaching/wblt/overview.htm

Han, J., & Singh, M. (2007). Getting world English speaking student teachers to the top of the class: Making hope for ethno-cultural diversity in teacher education robust. *Asia-Pacific Journal of Teacher Education, 35*(3), 291-309.

Healy, M. (2000). Developing the scholarship of teaching in higher education: A discipline-based approach. *Higher Education Research and Development, 19*(2), 169-189.

Herrington, J., Oliver, R. & Reeves, T. C. (2003). Patterns of engagement in authentic online learning environments. In A. Williamson, C. Gunn, A. Young and T. Clear (Eds), *Winds of Change in the Sea of Learning: Proceedings of the 19th Annual Conference of the Australasian Society for Computers in Learning in Tertiary Education*, 279-286. Auckland, New Zealand: UNITEC Institute of Technology.

Hofstede, G. (1997). *Cultures and organizations: Software of the mind.* London: McGraw Hill.

Hu, S., & Kuh, G. D. (2002). Being (dis)engaged in educationally purposeful activities: The influence of student and institutional characteristics. *Research in Higher Education*, 43, 555-576.

Jashke, K. (2007). DEEDS: The 'Design Education Sustainability' Project, First Phase. *Research News, Edition 17.* Retrieved from University of Brighton website: http://artsresearch.brighton.ac.uk/news/deeds

Johnston, P., Everard, M., Santillo, D., & Robert, K. H. (2007). Reclaiming the definition of sustainability. *Environmental science and pollution research international* 14(1), 60–66. Retrieved from http://link.springer.com/article/10.1065%2Fespr2007.01.375

Jones, S., Ladyshewsky, R., Oliver, B., Flavell, H., & Geoghegan, I. (2008). Academic leadership for course coordinators: Professional development program pilot results. In *Preparing for the graduate of 2015.* Proceedings of the 17th Annual Teaching Learning Forum, 30-31 January, 2008, Perth, Curtin University of Technology. Retrieved from http://otl.curtin.edu.au/tlf/tlf2008/contents-all.html

Kantanis, T. (2002). *Same or different: Issues that affect mature age undergraduate students' transition to university.* Paper presented to Pacific Rim First Year in Higher Education Conference Changing Agendas - Te Ao Hurihuri, held in Christchurch, New Zealand, July 4-8.

Kennedy, M. M. (2006). Knowledge and vision in teaching. *Journal of Teacher Education, 57(3),* 205. Retrieved from http://jte.sagepub.com/cgi/content/abstract/57/3/205

Kift, S. (2009). A transition pedagogy: The first year experience curriculum design symposium. *HERDSA News, 31*(1), 1-4.

Krause, K. L. (2005). Serious thoughts about dropping out in first year. *Studies in Learning, Evaluation and Development,* 2(3), 55-67.

Krause, K., Hartley, R., James, R. & McInnes, C. (2005). *The first year experience in Australian universities: Findings from a decade of national studies*. Department of Education, Science and Training. Canberra, Australia. Retrieved from http://www.dest.gov.au/sectors/higher_education/publications_resources/profiles/first_year_experience.htm

Krizek, K. J., Birnbaum, A. S., & Levinson, D. M. (2004). A schematic for focusing on youth in investigations of community design and physical activity. *American Journal of Health Promotion, 19*(1), 33-38.

Kuh, G. D. (2003). What we're learning about student engagement from NSSE: benchmarks for effective educational practices. *Change, 35*(2), 24-32.

—. (2005). Student engagement in the first year of college. In L. M. Upcraft, J. N. Gardner, & B. O. Barefoot (Eds.), *Challenging and supporting the first-year student: A handbook for improving the first year of college*. San Francisco: Jossey-Bass.

—. (2007). How to help students achieve. *The Chronicle of Higher Education, 53*(41), B12-13.

Lawrence, J. (2005). Reconceptualising attrition and retention: Integrating theoretical, research and student perspectives. *Studies in Learning, Evaluation and Development, 2*(3), 16-33.

—. (2007). Two models for facilitating cross-cultural communication and engagement. *International Journal of Diversity in Organisations, Communities and Nations, 6*(6), 73-82. Retrieved from Common Ground Publishing website: http://ijd.cgpublisher.com/product/pub.29/prod.423

Leask, B. (2004). *Transnational education and intercultural learning: Reconstructing the offshore teaching team to enhance Internationalisation*. Proceedings of the Australian Universities Quality Forum 2004 AUQA Occasional Publication.

Marklein, M. B. (2005, July 11). College 'swirling' muddies quality. *USA Today*.

McInnis C. (2003). *New realities of the student experience: How should universities respond?* Keynote address, 25th Annual Conference of the European Association for Institutional Research, Limerick, 24–27 August.

McLaughlin, P., & Mills, A. (2008). *Where shall the future student learn?* Student expectations of university facilities for teaching and learning. In Preparing for the graduate of 2015. Proceedings of the 17th Annual Teaching Learning Forum, 30-31 January 2008. Perth: Curtin University of Technology http://otl.curtin.edu.au/tlf/tlf2008/refereed/mclaughlin.html

Moore, J. (2005). Is higher education ready for transformative learning: A question explored in the study of sustainability. *Journal of transformative Education, 3*(1), 76-91.

National Survey of Student Engagement. (2000). *The NSSE 2000 report: National benchmarks of effective educational practice.* Bloomington, IN: Indiana University Center for Postsecondary Research.

Nelson, K. J., & Kift, S. M. (2005) Beyond curriculum reform: embedding the transition experience. In HERDSA 2005, 3-6 July, 2005, The University of Sydney, Sydney, Australia.

Oers, V. (1997). From context to contextualizing. *Learning and Instruction, 8*(6), 473-488.

Ramsden, P. (2003). *Learning to teach in higher education* (2nd ed.). London: Routledge.

Robson, J. (2006) *Teacher professionalism in further and higher education: Challenges to culture and practice.* London: Routledge.

Shulman, L. S. (1993). Teaching as community property. *Change* (Nov/Dec), 6-7.

—. (2004). *Teaching as community property: Essays on higher education.* San Francisco: Jossey, sustainable education, and problem-based learning in universities. *Journal of Transformative Education, 7*(3), 245-264.

Thomas, I., (2009). Critical thinking, transformative learning, sustainable education, and problem-based learning in universities. *Journal of Transformative Education, 7*(3), 245-264.

Tinto, V. (2005). Forward. In A. Seidman (Ed.), *College student retention: Formula for student success* (pp. ix–x). Westport, CT: American Council on Education/Praeger.

Trigwell, K., Martin, E., Benjamin, J. & Prosser, M. (2000). Scholarship of teaching. *Higher Education Research & Development, 19*(2), 155-169.

University of Southern Queensland. (2008a). Academic Calendar, Part 7: Teaching, research and scholarship section 7.1 *University calendar Issued 04/08* http://www.usq.edu.au/resources/71.pdf

—. (2008b). *Learning and teaching action kit: Flexible and open learning.* Retrieved from http://www.usq.edu.au/extrafiles/ltsu/LTActionKit/study_modules/FlexibleLearning.pdf

—. (2008c). Quality Policy: Guiding Principles for Learning and Teaching at USQ. Retrieved from University Calendar via http://www.usq.edu.au/corporateservices/calendar/part7.htm

—. (2009). *Strategic plan 2009-2013: Creating sustainable futures: Embracing the digital education revolution*. Toowoomba, Australia: Author.

Vosniadou, S. (1991). Are we ready for a psychology of learning and culture. *Learning and Instruction, 1*(3), 283-287.

Yorke, M. (2000). Smoothing the transition into higher education: What can be learned from student non-completion. *Journal of Institutional Research, 9*(1), 35-47.

Zepke, N., Leach, L., & Prebble, T. (2003). *Student support and its impact on learning outcomes*. Chapter presented at the HERDSA conference, Christchurch, July.

Chapter Three

Principles to Practice: Students' Learning Experiences

Lorelle Burton, Alice Brown, Ann Dashwood, and Jill Lawrence

Introduction

This chapter documents research examining students' perspectives on how well courses embedded the five principles described in Chapter Two: Sustainability, Engagement, Scholarship, Flexibility, and Contextual Learning. To do this, the current research team, a subgroup of the original transnational project (TP) team described in Chapter One, explored the views of a representative group of students about how academics embedded the five nominated teaching principles within their pedagogical practices. An ancillary goal of the study was to examine the reliability and validity of the newly developed *Best Practice Learning and Teaching Survey*.

This is the first of four chapters reporting the findings of the research conducted by the research team in 2007 to investigate the applicability of the five principles to both students and staff . The research process and student results are documented in Chapters Three (the quantitative results) and Four (the qualitative results) while Chapter Five specifically investigates the students' perceptions and experiences of the Contextual Learning principle. Chapter Six discusses the quantitative and qualitative staff results.

Background

As documented in Chapter One, the initial TP team fleshed out a USQ transnational pedagogy based on five principles (Crowther et al., 2005). This pedagogy was endorsed and disseminated by USQ Academic Board and Council in 2005 and 2006. Early in 2007, the authors, four members of the original TP team, developed a survey instrument to gather university wide perspectives from students and staff about the value, frequency, and extent to which learning and teaching at USQ is transnational. The survey items were based on the principles outlined in Chapter Two.

There were two versions of the survey: one for students and one for academic staff. The student version is shown in Appendix A. The student survey was administered online. Ethics approval was sought and obtained, and the student survey disseminated in Semester 2 and 3 of September, 2007. The academic staff survey was distributed in February 2008 and the results are reported in Chapter Six.

In the course of this research, the University's vision evolved from the focus on transnational education to an emphasis on sustainability and flexibility (USQ, 2009). The current research team, however, could accommodate this change, after much consultation across the University, because of the continued relevance of the five principles–two of which were explicitly prioritised in the new vision. The transnational pedagogy survey was recalibrated to examine "best practice" in learning and teaching (see Chapter Two). The aim was to measure student and staff perspectives of the five principles thought to underpin good practice in learning and teaching.

Method

Participants

A total of 944 (of the 2551 actively enrolled) undergraduate students enrolled in at least one course in Semesters 2 or 3 in 2007 completed the online survey, resulting in a response rate of 37.0%. Of these, 50.21% were female and 49.78% were male. The participants' ages ranged from 16 to 82 with a mean age of 31.6 ($SD = 10.9$). With regards to study location, 37.3% identified as local (Toowoomba and surrounding regions), 43.2% were from other regions of Queensland (metropolitan and regional areas included), 12.5% were from other states of Australia, and 7% resided in other countries. Most students (91.5%) identified English as the language spoken at home, with the only other primary language of note being Chinese (2.5%) which incorporated both Mandarin and Cantonese. However, of the 8% that did not speak English at home, 6% indicated that English was their second language.

Students' reports of time since last study indicated that 37.5% of were continuing students, 28.2% had not studied in the last 1 to 4 years, 9.5% had not studied in the last 5 to 7 years, while 24.8% had not studied for more than seven years. Most (58.9%) were new to distance education and, of those who had studied externally before, 27.5% had studied at USQ. Almost a third (30.4%) of the sample began their program of study in 2007, while most had begun their current study program between 2004 and 2007.

Table 3.1 shows the frequency data for three key demographic variables: Age, Faculty, and Location of Study.

Table 3.1: Frequencies for Age (Scaled), Faculty, and Study Location

Age	N	Faculty	N	Location	N
<=20 yrs	160	Arts	156	Toowoomba	352
21-30 yrs	336	Business	206	Regional Qld	112
31-40 yrs	256	Education	180	Coastal Qld	120
41-50 yrs	139	Engineering & Surveying	127	Brisbane	175
51-60 yrs	43	Other	12	Another State	118
60+ yrs	10	Sciences	263	Another Country	66
Total	944	Total	944	Total	943

Data from the student survey were collated electronically and scored and analysed using the Statistical Package for Social Scientists (SPSS – standard version 17.0).

Instrument

The study collected both quantitative and qualitative data using a self-report survey (see Appendix A). Participants were asked to determine (a) the extent to which each of the five teaching principles exemplified good practice in higher education, and (b) the extent to which these principles were embedded within the current learning and teaching practices and materials. The survey used a combination of forced-choice and open questions to address these *what, how, and why* issues. Care was taken to avoid pre-disposing respondents' answers to ensure they could interpret all questions without ambiguity. A pilot study was conducted with student and staff focus groups to validate the survey instrument. The feedback obtained from focus groups was applied to both surveys.

Procedure

Students were invited to participate via email using the USQ remailer system. The email provided a web link to the survey. Staff teaching into programs posted this same message to their course discussion groups. All participants had to provide their informed consent before participating. As an incentive, student participants could have their name entered in a random draw for a $50 USQ Bookshop Voucher.

Students completed the survey using an electronic survey system, accessed online via a secured website, developed by Psychology Technical Services at USQ. The study aimed to include all undergraduate students (including on-campus domestic, distance, and international students) enrolled in programs offered at USQ. The sample included both on-campus and distance education student cohorts and comprised students from Australia, Singapore, Malaysia and elsewhere, at various stages of their degrees.

The student survey comprised nine items exploring participants' demographics (e.g., age, gender, languages spoken, location of study, and previous study) and 44 questions measuring the following five principles, using the following definitions:

1. The Sustainability principle: the ability to meet present needs within a code of ethical practice without compromising the ability to meet future needs.
2. The Engagement principle: means participating in interactive exchanges of knowledge; collaborating by working creatively in partnerships, student to student, teacher to student.
3. The Scholarship principle: embodies respect for diverse learning and teaching styles; upholding excellence and integrity of scholarship across disciplines.
4. The Flexibility principle: the provision of supportive, inclusive and flexible learning environments.
5. The Contextual Learning principle: recognising and valuing students' backgrounds and contexts.

Of the 44 items, 29 elicited quantitative data and 15 qualitative data (unreported). The quantitative items typically required a 5-point (1 = *least important/frequent*; 5 = *most important/freque*nt) Likert-scale response, or in some instances, a *yes/no* response. For each principle, students were requested to respond (*yes/no*) to whether they were able to identify a course (subject) that would reflect the application of that principle within their study program. For example, for the Engagement principle, students were asked "can you identify a course that helped your learning by providing opportunities for engagement?" The 15 qualitative items then asked students to specifically identify courses that had contributed to their understanding of each of the five principles and to provide any relevant comments. Analysis of these qualitative items is beyond the scope of this current chapter. For each principle, students had to indicate how important the principle had been to their learning (Importance), how frequently the principle had been applied in their studies (Frequency), and how much the principle had enhanced their learning (Knowledge Extension).

Results

Mean total scale scores were computed for each principle and Table 3.3 shows the descriptive statistics. As shown in the table, the Sustainability, Engagement and Contextual Learning total scales each demonstrated satisfactory internal consistency. The reliability estimates for the Scholarship and Flexibility scales were acceptable for further analyses; however, results for these variables should be interpreted with caution. Overall, students' responses indicated a general agreement that the each of the five principles were relevant to their studies.

Table 3.2: Descriptive Statistics for the Five Principle Scale Scores (N= 944)

Variable	M	SD	α	No. of items
Sustainability	3.71	0.65	.88	9
Engagement	3.85	0.65	.74	5
Scholarship	3.84	0.57	.62	4
Flexibility	3.94	0.62	.60	3
Contextual Learning	3.16	0.87	.76	3

As shown in Table 3.2., these five principle variables were highly intercorrelated (.36 < r < .61, p < .01). Table 3.3 shows the descriptive statistics for the extent to which students could identify each principle in their courses.

Table 3.3: Yes/No percentages for evidence of Five Principles' application in S2 2007 courses

Responses	Sustainability	Engagement	Scholarship	Flexibility	Contextual Learning
Yes	51.4%	70.0%	68.2%	54.8%	35.5%
No	48.6%	30.0%	31.8%	45.2%	64.5%

As shown in Table 3.3, the Contextual Learning principle recorded more *no* than *yes* responses – in fact nearly twice as many–while the other four Principles had a greater percentage of *yes* responses. In contrast, for both the Engagement and Scholarship principles, nearly twice as many students endorsed *yes* rather than *no*. This indicates that students perceive these two principles to be strongly embedded in course content. In contrast, the Sustainability and Flexibility principles appear to be less evident.

Paired t-test comparisons (df = 943) for the Contextual Learning principle with the other four principles (Sustainability t= -8.48; Engagement t= -18.77; Scholarship t= -18.2; Flexibility t= -11.11) all indicated those four principles' mean responses were significantly different at the .001 level of probability from the mean for the Contextual Learning principle. This indicates that students did not recognise the Contextual Learning principle as frequently as the other four principles.

Consistent with the *Yes/No* responses comparison, the above data indicate that the Contextual Learning principle received less endorsement from students in comparison to the other four principles. For example, paired t-test comparisons were computed for the Contextual Learning principle with each of the other four principles. All four t-test comparisons revealed significant mean differences, as follows: between Contextual Learning and Sustainability, t (943) = 18.54, p < .01; Contextual Learning and Engagement t (943) = -23.25, p < .01; Contextual Learning and Scholarship t (943) = -24.94, p < .01; and Contextual Learning and Flexibility t (943) = -28.01, p < .01. Together, these results indicate that student ratings for Importance, Frequency and Knowledge Extension for Contextual Learning were less than those for the other four principles.

Relationships among the five principles and the main background variables were explored via correlation procedures. Gender, Age (Scaled), and Faculty did not have significant relationships with any of the five principles. However, Location of Study and Previous External Study did exhibit significant relationships with three principles–Location of Study with Sustainability and Engagement; Previous External Study with Flexibility. These interrelationships are presented in Table 3.4.

Table 3.4: Correlations for Five Principles with Two Background Variables (N=944)

	Variable	1	2	3	4	5	6	7
1.	Location of Study		.08*	-.09**	-.20**	-.03	-.03	-.04
2.	Previous External Study			-.05	-.03	-.05	-.08*	-.06
3.	Sustainability				.45**	.46**	.40**	.36**
4.	Engagement					.48**	.48**	.35**
5.	Scholarship						.61**	.43**
6.	Flexibility							.41**
7.	Contextual Learning							

Note. ** $p < .001$, * $p < .05$ (two-tailed)

The three significant inter-correlations observed in Table 3.4 were subjected to paired t-tests analyses to explore further their relationships. All three relationships were significant at the .001 probability level– Location of Study with Sustainability: $t(943) = -15.23$; Location of Study with Engagement: $t(943) = -16.93$; and Previous External Study with Flexibility: $t(943) = -86.35$. Thus, it could be deduced that, for students in the sample, studying in Toowoomba or other areas of Queensland was significantly related to higher ratings for the Sustainability and Engagement principles. Similarly, it would appear that having studied externally previously was significantly linked to higher ratings for the Flexibility principle.

Mean total scale scores for Importance of the principle, Frequency of the principle and Knowledge Extension through the principle were then calculated (see Table 3.6). The mean Importance, Frequency, and Knowledge Extension scores for each of the five principles are also shown in the table.

Table 3.5: Descriptive Statistics for Importance, Frequency, and Knowledge Extension Measures

Variable	Importance of the Principle		Frequency of the Principle		Knowledge Extension through the Principle	
	M	SD	M	SD	M	SD
Total Scale	4.08	0.55	3.50	0.64	3.52	0.59
Sustainability	4.21*	0.69	3.61*	0.85	3.31*	0.87
Engagement	4.05*	0.76	3.63*	0.88	3.89*	0.88
Scholarship	4.18*	0.76	3.39*	0.87	3.60*	0.85
Flexibility	4.24*	0.79	3.59*	0.90	3.98*	0.81
Contextual Learning	3.39	1.06	2.93*	1.04	2.93*	1.04

Note. * indicates a significant mean difference as compared with Context using a paired t-test.

There were apparent differences between the three teaching application variables, and paired t-test procedures were used to further explore these differences. It was found that Importance was significantly different from both Frequency, $t(943) = 27.95$, $p < .001$, and Knowledge Extension $t(943) = 33.3$, $p < .001$, respectively. This indicates that students rated, on average, each of the five principles as being important in their studies; however, they did not perceive them to be frequently applied in their courses nor to enhance their learning in the course. For example, the Contextual Learning principle was not rated as highly as Flexibility for Importance, $t(943) = 24.27$, $p < .001$; Contextual Learning was rated less than Engagement for Frequency, $t(943) = 19.66$, $p < .001$; Contextual Learning was rated less than Flexibility for Knowledge Extent, $t(943) = -25.88$, $p < .001$. Other mean differences are also evident in the table.

Summary

Across the five principles, 56% (for Contextual Learning) to 75% (for Engagement) of all surveyed students provided statements about the presence, or absence, of the principle within their courses. Students' responses about the good practice teaching principles were three to six times more likely to be positive than negative, except for the Contextual Learning principle where positive and negative instances were almost exactly the same. Highest positive instances (85% of the principle's responses) were recorded for Scholarship while the highest negative instances (50%) were for the Contextual Learning principle.

Discussion

The student survey demonstrated adequate internal consistency and had good face validity. However, further revision of the scale is recommended, including enabling students to explain more fully their faculty and/or program of study in order to tease out comparisons between local students, regional students and interstate and international students. Two key background variables, Location of Study and Previous External Study showed findings of interest with the five principles and require further consideration.

Survey Instrument

Results from the present investigation supported both propositions to a considerable extent. Survey variables' mean responses, on a 5-point Likert Scale (1 being *least*; 5 being *most important, frequent, or extensive*), ranged from 2.92 to 4.26. All responses were well above the survey mid-point of 2.5 and a greater percentage of students endorsed ratings of 3 (*a moderate amount)* and 4 (*a great amount*) for each variable. These scores reveal that the survey was indeed measuring what it was intended to measure, indicating that the instrument had good face validity. Furthermore, inter-relationships among the 15 main variables (each representing a *Teaching Application-Principle* combination) all showed highly significant relationships, confirming good internal consistency between and across survey variables.

Five Teaching Principles

Survey results indicated strong endorsement from students for the Sustainability, Engagement, Scholarship, and Flexibility principles within course teaching. The Flexibility principle was rated as very important, reflecting the high proportion of distance students who study at USQ who often need to juggle work and study commitments. In contrast, the Contextual Learning principle received significantly lower rating scores than the other four, across all three teaching applications. Similarly, all principles recorded more *yes* than *no* responses from students except the Contextual Learning principle which recorded as many *no* as *yes* responses. Nevertheless, the overall mean response rate for the Contextual Learning Principle ($M = 3.16$) was still higher than the midpoint survey response of 2.5. The finding indicates that students still saw this principle operating within USQ teaching practices, although they could not identify examples to the same extent as the other four principles. This could partly reflect how the Contextual Learning principle example was worded. Only a very brief explanation was provided, stating that context "recognises and values students' background and contexts". Perhaps this definition is insufficient and students need better guidance in recognising and valuing this concept in teaching practices. Alternatively, students might simply believe the Contextual Learning principle is not as prevalent in USQ teaching practices as the other four principles. Findings from the qualitative data may shed further light. Other implications here might be whether lecturers did not value this Contextual Learning principle as highly as the other principles and therefore provided fewer examples in their teaching? As Chapter Four later argues, it would seem that these students did not encounter the principle in action in their courses and also did not understand the concept and relevance of context within their study programs. And yet, students rated the importance of course material recognising and valuing their background and context quite highly.

Overall, it appears that the students in this study believe that the five teaching principles are important aspects of their learning. A key finding, however, is that students further believe these principles were only moderately likely to be found in their learning materials or to extend their knowledge acquisition in their courses.

Implications

If, as it seems, students deem these five principles as important, but do not see their application as strongly evident in teaching practices, USQ could explore the possibility of incorporating professional development programs about these principles for staff who are unaware of them or under-using them. Results from the present survey could then be used as a pre-test against which to compare results after professional development.

Further research at USQ could employ this survey in a pre-test/post-test research design. It could be used in comparison studies with equal numbers for Faculty comparisons, for age comparisons, for locality comparisons, and even gender comparisons. It would also be important to find out how international students living overseas relate to the application of the principles. Finally, definitions of the five principles could be "tightened up" and described in more detail (as in the case of Contextual learning principle) to avoid possible confusion.

Conclusion

This practical study provided good evidence for the importance and application of the five principles within USQ teaching and learning practices. The strong recognition of the Scholarship principle raises further questions–why was it recognised much more strongly in teaching processes than the other principles? Is it because this principle has traditionally been expected in university teaching and therefore students could identify its characteristics more readily? Did lecturers provide stronger evidence of this principle in their teaching than they did for the other principles? And why was the Contextual learning principle less highly rated in the survey, less likely to be identified in surveyed courses, and less likely to have elicited positive instances from students who proffered reasons for the presence or absence of the principle in particular courses? One explanation is the Contextual learning principle is a bit too new for students to fully understand or was not well explained in the survey. Another is that lecturers do not value it as highly as the other principles and therefore provided fewer examples in their teaching. Finally, perhaps students do not value it as highly as the other principles. It appears from the texts detailing negative responses, that these students did not encounter the Contextual learning principle in action in their courses and also did not understand the concept and its relevance within their study programs. And yet, students rated the importance of course material recognising and valuing their background and context quite highly. Further analysis is warranted.

Overall, the research team considered that the current student survey provided good evidence for the importance and application of the five principles within teaching and learning practices. The survey also proved to be a robust instrument that could be useful for future professional development and research purposes at USQ and indeed elsewhere in the university sector.

References

Crowther, F., Behjat, N., Birch, D., Brodie, L., Burton, L., Connors, B., Cretchley, P., Dashwood, A., Hoey, A., Lawrence, J., Brown, A., Locke, J., Maroulis, J., Smith, A., & Wood, D. (2005). *Transnational pedagogy: A stimulus paper for consideration by the USQ professional community.* Unpublished manuscript, University of Southern Queensland, Toowoomba, Australia.

University of Southern Queensland. (2009). *Strategic plan 2009-2013: Creating sustainable futures: Embracing the digital education revolution.* Toowoomba, Australia: Author.

Appendix A
Best Practice in Learning and Teaching: Transnational Pedagogy

Student Version

Personal Details

Gender	Male Female
Location of Study	Local Toowoomba
	Regional Queensland
	Coastal Queensland
	Brisbane
	Another state
	Another country
Language used at home	
Other languages spoken	
Number of years since previous study	Continuous
	1-4
	5-7
	More than 7
Age	18-21 years
	22 – 24 years
	25-34 years
	35 + years
Have you ever studied externally before?	Yes (Where?)
	No

USQ values flexible learning approaches to education. That includes a flexible and responsive approach to learning and teaching for students whoever and wherever they are.

Completing this survey will help us to gain student and teacher perspectives on best practice learning and teaching which is responsive in global and local contexts.

We believe that five principles form the basis for flexible learning and teaching. The meaning of each principle is explained for the purpose of this research.

1. **The Sustainability Principle**: USQ embraces the Sustainability Principle, the ability to meet present needs within a code of ethical practice without compromising the ability to meet future needs.
2. **The Engagement Principle**: USQ fosters engagement and collaboration. Engagement means participating in interactive exchanges of knowledge. Collaboration means working creatively in partnerships, student to student, teacher to student.
3. **The Scholarship Principle**: USQ respects diverse learning and teaching styles and upholds excellence and integrity of scholarship across disciplines.
4. **The Flexibility Principle**: USQ accepts individual and collective responsibility in providing supportive, inclusive and flexible learning environments.
5. **The Contextual Learning Principle**: USQ recognises and values students' backgrounds and contexts.

....

QUESTIONS FOR *STUDENTS*
To answer the following questions please indicate your response by selecting the appropriate number in the scale.

The Sustainability Principle: USQ embraces the Sustainability Principle, the ability to meet present needs within a code of ethical practice without compromising the ability to meet future needs.

1. How important is it that your program addresses:
    (a) *current professional issues?* [1-5 VALUE]
    (b) *ethical codes of practice?* [1-5 VALUE]
    (c) *future practices* [1-5 VALUE]

2. How often does your program refer to:
   (a) *current professional issues?* [1-5 VALUE]
   (b) *ethical codes of practice?* [1-5 VALUE]
   (c) *future practices* [1-5 VALUE]

3. To what extent does your program contribute to your knowledge of:
   (a) *current professional issues?* [1-5 VALUE]
   (b) *ethical codes of practice?* [1-5 VALUE]
   (c) *future practices* [1-5 VALUE]

4. Can you identify a course that contributes to your understanding of issues related to sustainability?
   YES–course code/s.....If yes, please explain how that understanding was developed:
   NO–...If no, please provide a comment:

The Engagement Principle: USQ fosters engagement and collaboration. Engagement means participating in interactive exchanges of knowledge. Collaboration means working creatively in partnerships, student to student, teacher to student.

1. How important is it that your program enables you to engage with the content and interact with others (e.g., fellow students, staff, and community members)? [1-5 VALUE]

2. How often do you have opportunities to engage with course content and with others? [1-5 FREQUENCY]

3. To what extent does being engaged help you to learn? [1-5 LEARNING OUTCOME]

4. Can you identify a course that helped your learning by providing opportunities for engagement?
   YES–course code/s.....If yes, please explain how that was achieved:
   NO–...If no, please provide a comment:

The Scholarship Principle: USQ respects diverse learning and teaching styles. It upholds excellence and integrity of scholarship across USQ disciplines.

1. How important is it that your program respects and values the way you learn? [1-5 VALUE]

2. How important is it that your teachers understand and cater for your learning style? [1-5 VALUE]

3. How often is your learning style accommodated for in your learning materials? [1-5 FREQUENCY]

4. To what extent do the learning materials facilitate your learning? [1-5 LEARNING OUTCOMES]

5. Can you identify a course, learning activity, or assessment task that enhanced your learning experience?[1-5 LEARNING OUTCOMES]
YES–course code/s.....If yes, please explain how that was achieved:
NO–...If no, please provide a comment:

The Flexibility Principle: USQ accepts individual and collective responsibility in providing supportive, inclusive and flexible learning environments.

1. How important is it that your program provides supportive, inclusive and flexible learning environments? [1-5 VALUE]

2. How often do your teachers provide learning environments that are supportive, inclusive and flexible? [1-5 FREQUENCY]

3. To what extent do supportive, inclusive and flexible learning environments enhance your learning? [1-5 LEARNING OUTCOMES]

4. Can you identify a course, learning activity or assessment task that enhanced your learning by providing a supportive, inclusive and flexible learning environment?
YES–course code/s.....If yes, please explain how that was achieved:
NO–...If no, please provide a comment:

The Contextual Learning Principle: USQ recognises and values students' backgrounds and contexts.

1. How important is it that the course materials recognise and value your background and context? [1-5 VALUE]

2. How often is your background and context acknowledged in your course materials? [1-5 FREQUENCY]

3. To what extent does considering your background and context enhance your learning? [1-5 LEARNING OUTCOME]

4. Can you identify a course, learning activity or assessment task that enhanced your learning by considering your background and context? YES–course code/s…..If yes, please explain how that was achieved: NO–…If no, please provide a comment:

Thank-you for completing this survey. The information we obtain from this survey will help us to better meet students' learning needs by increasing our understanding of those needs and how they can be met.

CHAPTER FOUR

DELVING DEEPER:
EXPLORING STUDENTS' LEARNING
EXPERIENCES OF THE FIVE PRINCIPLES
OF PEDAGOGY

JILL LAWRENCE, ANN DASHWOOD,
ALICE BROWN, AND LORELLE BURTON

Introduction

Chapter Three described the background, aim, method, and participants as well as the demographic and quantitative results obtained from the *Best Practice Learning and Teaching* student survey. It became evident that students strongly recognised the Scholarship principle in practice; in contrast, the Contextual Learning principle received significantly lower rating scores than the other four principles across all three teaching applications. Chapter Four documents the qualitative results obtained from the student survey. The qualitative component of the survey included 15 questions asking students to specifically identify courses that had contributed to their understanding of each of the five principles–Sustainability, Engagement, Scholarship, Flexibility, and Contextual Learning–and to provide comments on how this was, or was not, achieved. An excel chart was used to collate students' responses into categories as binary qualitative data sets. The findings reported here echo and enrich those observed for the quantitative data in each of the five principles.

The following sections discuss in detail the qualitative results for each of the principles. Later Chapters Eight and Nine link the findings discussed here to the more enduring principles, for example, considering how the principles have adapted in response to current learning and teaching priorities and to the shifting contexts of the higher education sector.

Method

Participants

A total of 944 undergraduate students enrolled in at least one course in Semesters 2 or 3 in 2007 completed the online student survey. As outlined in Chapter Three, the sample comprised 474 females and 470 males. The participants' ages ranged from 16 to 82 with a mean age of 31.6 ($SD = 10.9$). More than one third of the sample (37.3%) identified as local students (i.e., based in Toowoomba and surrounding regions), 43.2% were from other regions of Queensland (i.e., metropolitan and regional areas), 12.5% were located in other states of Australia, and 7% were based internationally.

Instrument

Of the 44 items included in the student survey, 15 elicited qualitative data. For each principle, students were asked (*yes/no*) if they could identify a course (subject) that reflected that principle being applied. Students were then asked to provide written explanations for their *yes/no* choice. Two open-ended requests followed: "If yes, please explain how this was achieved"; "If no, please provide a comment". The qualitative data arising from these explanations were collated and analysed in the following manner. For example, for the Engagement principle, students were asked "can you identify a course that helped your learning by providing opportunities for engagement?" The 15 qualitative items then asked students to specifically identify courses that had contributed to their understanding of each of the five principles and to provide any relevant comments.

Results

Data Analysis

Qualitative data from the survey were collated electronically and scored and analysed using the NVivo Statistical Package. A number of steps occurred to assign meaning to the qualitative open-ended section of the transnational survey. During the initial phase of analysis, common themes in student responses generated categories. At face-to-face meetings, the transnational project research team established a degree of congruence of interpreting the students' responses by category. "Modified" random sampling was used to select 91 sets of responses (10% of the data set) across the five principles that were presented as typed responses on Excel sheets. From the instances reported the researchers identified themes, proposed category names, and reached consensus on titles for the coding. This method aimed at establishing reliability, ensuring consistency, and eliminating duplication. A reliability index of 81% congruence was established on coding the instances of Scholarship. Having established codes for the many themes, the three researchers each coded 300 sets of student responses on each of the five principles to complete the full data set. In cases of multiple messages from individual students, they applied multiple codes. NVivo software was used to collate those responses into the categories as binary qualitative data sets. Table 4.1 provides a summary of students' responses across the five principles.

Table 4.1: Summary of Students' Responses

Code Names	Nodes	References
Sustainability No	16	136
Sustainability Yes	**14**	**681**
Engagement No	16	148
Engagement Yes	**17**	**770**
Scholarship No	18	238
Scholarship Yes	**17**	**503**
Flexibility No	13	169
Flexibility Yes	**15**	**499**
Contextual Learning No	14	488
Contextual Learning Yes	**14**	**502**

All surveyed students provided statements about the presence, or absence, of the principles within their course/s for the surveyed teaching semester. Responses were three to six times more likely to be positive than negative, except for the Contextual Learning principle where positive and negative instances were almost exactly the same. The highest positive instances (85% of the principle's responses) were recorded for Scholarship while the highest negative instances (50%) were for Contextual Learning principle. Most positive remarks emphasised teachers' attributes (i.e., professionalism; strong ethical principles, beliefs, and values; positive interaction/collaboration with other teachers and students; and empathy, support and understanding of students' work/life situations), teaching skills, and quality course organisation, materials, and resources. For a number of students, negative instances mirrored positive remarks insofar as these evaluations remarked on poor teaching skills, problems with course materials and lack of understanding of students' needs. However, most students who evaluated negatively reported no evidence of the principle/s in their courses. They also indicated no understanding of the meaning of the principle, that the principle was not relevant to their learning, and that it was too early in the course to identify the principle. Each principle is now discussed in turn.

Sustainability Principle

In the student survey, the Sustainability principle was defined as follows: "USQ embraces the Sustainability principle, the ability to meet present needs within a code of ethical practice without compromising the ability to meet future needs." Overall, 65% of the 944 surveyed students provided 661 exemplars (71% positive; 20% negative) of the Sustainability principle in practice. Relevant comments were selected from all Sustainability responses and categorised. Following each category (in italics) student comments are provided. Identified positive instances included:

1. *Ethical practice*: By developing credibility of profession/s; by maintaining professional standards; through using case studies in ethical practice.
2. *Materials*: Providing of resources and modules dedicated to sustainability in the environment and ethical practice.
3. *Real life examples*, including applications to real-life situations, providing an understanding of the global economy, impact on the lives of people.
4. *Strategic teaching,* including discussions, case studies, authentic contexts relating to Sustainability, teaching for life-long learning.
5. Topics, projects concerning future and *current sustainable practices*, population change, scope for sustainable change.

6. *Local and global issues* within teaching practices, including issues such as community development, business issues, enhancement plans.
7. *Relevant assessment*, for example, assignments, topics, projects referring to sustainability.
8. *Other: G*eneral statements advocating greater awareness of sustainability, future learning needs, life-long learning needs, and ethical practice.

Interestingly, the data did not nominate technological practices. This is in contrast to Gosper et al. (2008), who found that students feel technological practices lead to them achieving better (i.e., more sustainable) results, making it easier to learn. Gosper et al. (2008) concluded that academic teachers need to experiment with new technologies to make their teaching practices "more effective and sustainable in the longer term" (p. 11). However, the data–for example, students' nomination of real life examples, discussions, case studies and authentic contexts–confirm Jashke's (2007) conclusions that sustainability is an ethical as much as a "practical-technical" challenge, which should operate within a comprehensive, holistic framework and should be (a) specific to context, (b) evolving, and (c) an open-ended process.

Responses from students who did not identify a course in which the Sustainability principle was evident were also categorised. Following each category (in italics) student comments are provided:

1. *Not identified* in courses: Only talked about but not taught; practices taught that we will not use when we graduate; have not heard the word "sustainability" before at USQ.
2. *Too early* in nominated courses to detect the Sustainability principle in teaching practices.
3. *Don't understand*: Don't understand the concept of Sustainability; this (concept) is complicated.
4. *Not sure:* Sustainability principle was not evident in teaching practice/s.
5. *Not relevant:* It was not the course role to provide Sustainability; the issue was not particularly important; not of concern (for) learning; no need to contemplate the future requirements of course.
6. *Other*: For example, statement is too broad; courses too theoretical; Sustainability is a personal thought (construct).

The relatively recent appearance of the Sustainability principle on the higher education agenda may shape these negative responses. For example, USQ only recently added sustainable practices to its graduate qualities, with course specifications just beginning to address the quality in their objectives in late 2009. The perceived lack of sustainability in courses may also reflect Kennedy's (2006) acknowledgement that academic research into sustainable teaching and learning practice is still in its infancy. Overall, the data suggests that students did not appear to have a good understanding of the concept, a finding which poses questions about the validity of students' responses about this principle in particular. Categorised positive and negative instances of the Sustainability principle are presented in Table 4.2.

Table 4.2: Positive and Negative Instances of Reporting Sustainability Principle Categories

Sustainability Category	Positive Instances	%	Sustainability Category	Negative Instances	%
1. Ethics	109	23	1. Not identified in course	39	20.5
2. Materials/ resources	101	21	2. Too early in course	36	19
3. Examples	98	21	3. Don't understand	33	17.5
4. Strategic teaching	57	12	4. Not sure	28	15
5. Future	46	10	5. Not relevant	14	7
6. Local and global	23	5	6. Other	40	21
7. Assessment	19	4			
8. Other	18	4			
Instances	471		Instances	190	

In summary, at least two-thirds of students who reported positive instances of the Sustainability principle considered that observed ethical standards in lecturers' teaching and professional practices, strategic use of ethical and sustainable teaching materials (including real life teaching examples) were important ways to engage them. However, a small number believed the issues of ethics and sustainability were irrelevant or not addressed in their courses.

Engagement Principle

In the student survey, the Engagement principle was defined as follows: "USQ fosters engagement and collaboration. Engagement means participating in interactive exchanges of knowledge. Collaboration means working creatively in partnerships, student to student, teacher to student." When asked to describe how they could, or could not, identify the Engagement principle in their courses, 75% of all surveyed students provided 651 instances (83% positive; 17% negative). Students' evaluations provided a range of insights into their understandings of the nature of engagement which were categorised in the following ways. For identified instances:

1. *Interaction and collaboration*, for example, class discussions, open discussions; collaboration among both students and lecturers.
2. *Strategic organisation,* including tutorials, team based activities, problem-solving, critiques, small classes, residential schools, group work, and study groups.
3. *Use of information communication technologies (ICTs),* in particular WebCT, course home pages, StudyDesk, discussion boards, Knowledge Gardens, and blog posts.
4. *Course materials and resources*, for example, course layouts and topics.
5. *Quality assessment processes,* including CMA tests, quizzes, and projects.
6. *Professionalism;* for example, well prepared tutors, weekly consultations (online), and supportive lecturers.
7. *Personal interactions*, for example, relating to (students') own life situations and reducing fears re study.
8. *Practicum*, such as clinical placements, class activities, and practical activities.

These results confirm Kift's (2009) conclusion that good curriculum design enacts an engaging and involving pedagogy. Kift (2009) argued that the Australasian Survey of Student Engagement (AUSSE; Coates, 2007; Radloff & Coates, 2009) now provides clear guidance around the "activities and conditions likely to generate high quality learning" (ACER, 2008, p. vi) and evidences that "all aspects of engagement have a strong positive relationship with a range of general, specific, social, personal, ethical and interpersonal capabilities" (ACER, 2008, p. ix). The student survey results echo Kift's (2009) and Pascarella and Terenzini's (2005) views that innovative, active, collaborative, and constructivist instructional approaches shape learning much more powerfully than do conventional lecture-discussion and text-based approaches. Kuh, Gruce, Shoup, Kinzie, and Gonyea (2008, p. 21) noted that "when I am asked, what one thing we can do to enhance student engagement and increase student success? I now have an answer: make it possible for every student to participate in *at least two high impact activities* during his or her undergraduate program, one in the first year, and one taken later in relation to the major field."

These views resonate in the negative perceptions about the courses' capacities for engagement. Poor communication rated highly. However other comments reflect the complex lives students lead in a regional university juggling jobs, children, and studies. Lack of time was provided as a factor, for example. Responses from students, who could not identify at least one course in which engagement was evident, focused mainly on the following reasons:

1. *Poor communication*, including a poor level of communication, limited evidence of engagement, no follow-through or communication from lecturers.
2. *Learning styles issues* including discomfort with course study desk discussions.
3. *Perceived lack of time* to engage or too little time to engage.
4. *Too early in the course* to assess this principle
5. *Not sure.*
6. *Other.*

Both positive and negative instances of engagement are presented in Table 4.3 below.

Table 4.3: Positive and Negative Instances of Reporting Engagement Principle Categories

Engagement Category	Positive Instances	%	Engagement Category	Negative Instances	%
1. Interaction and collaboration	134	25	1. Poor communication	19	17
2. Strategic organisation	133	25	2. Learning styles issues	29	25
3. Use of ICTs	124	23	3. No time to engage	6	5
4. Course materials and resources	12	2	4. Too early in the course to assess	14	13
5. Assessment	25	5	5. Not sure	9	8
6. Professionalism	56	10	6. Other	34	32
7. Personal	17	3			
8. Practicum	39	7			
Total Instances	540		Total Instances	111	

Thus students considered that teachers' interactions with students, their professionalism, and their ability to strategically organise tutorials, study activity, group work, and course materials were all important ways to engage them. Their testimonies endorsed the presence of the Engagement principle in their studies. However, a small number of students reported that poor communication within some courses, learning style issues, and study time constraints worked against engagement with staff and with course work.

Scholarship Principle

In the student survey, the Scholarship principle was defined as follows: "USQ respects diverse learning and teaching styles. It upholds excellence and integrity of scholarship across USQ disciplines." The data revealed that 72% of the 944 students described 779 instances (73% positive; 27% negative) of the presence of the Scholarship principle. Students' positive and negative evaluations relating to the Scholarship principle were categorised as follows. Following each category (in italics) student comments are provided. The identified instances included:

1. *Organisation* of course delivery by means of residential schools, recorded lectures, oral assignments, case studies, hands-on activities, and the study schedule.
2. *Quality of course material*, including how the resources and content were managed to make them accessible for learning and for assessment.
3. *Appropriate assessment*, including diverse, oral, and online-tasks.
4. Selection of *real world exemplars* in the courses.
5. *Academic skills*, including research skills development; focus activities; and task-based ethics.
6. A belief that their *learning styles* were considered.
7. *Use of ICTs,* in particular interactive software and online discussions.
8. *Quality teaching styles* that enhanced learning.

Negative responses from students encompassed the following reasons:

1. *Poor teaching styles,* including a poor level of communication.
2. Personal *learning style issues* not catered for by lecturers.
3. Scholarship *not evident* in courses.
4. *Too early* in program/course to identify the Scholarship principle.
5. *Workload too heavy* to observe evidence of Scholarship principle.
6. Scholarship principle *not relevant,* or not consistent or transferrable in course/s.

Both positive and negative instances were categorised and are presented in Table 4.4 below.

Table 4.4: Positive and Negative Instances of Reporting Scholarship Principle Categories

Scholarship Category	Positive Instances	%	Scholarship Category	Negative Instances	%
1. Organisation	205	31	1. Poor teaching style	46	41
2. Materials/ resources	107	16	2. Learning Style	17	15
3. Assessment	103	16	3. Not evident	18	16
4. Real world examples	63	10	4. Too early in course/s	13	11
5. Academic skills	49	7	5. Workload	6	5
6. Learning style	57	9	6. Relevance etc	4	4
7. ICT	51	8	7. Other	9	8
8. Teaching quality	31	5			
Total Instances	666		Total Instances	113	

As with the Engagement principle, students identified that the main means of fostering the Scholarship principle involved teachers' abilities to design relevant study tasks and course materials, to appropriately use ICTs, and to exhibit effective academic skills and teaching qualities. At least two-thirds of the students recorded positive instances of the Scholarship principle. Again, a small minority reflected negatively on some lecturers' teaching styles, arguing that learning style issues and high workloads constituted barriers to good scholarship.

Students' positive evidence confirms Shulman's (2004) argument that students respond positively to their teachers' ability to make public their knowledge of notions of scholarship, by sharing and building knowledge. They reported understanding the notion of scholarship in a number of ways that are either not prominent in the literature, or in ways that refer explicitly to personal learning. Academics typically view the research into teaching and learning within the disciplines as scholarship (Trigwell, Martin, Benjamin, & Prosser, 2000). Participants in this survey however focused initially on their teachers' consideration of the learning environment being established "through" the discipline rather than learning "of" the discipline. Enhancing learning opportunities appears to be very important for students.

Management of the learning environment and the teachers' ability to structure course content, and to discuss and share insights into the academic disciplines were most often stated as indicators of the Scholarship principle. Opportunities to engage with their peers and their teachers who established communication through technology and face-to-face encounters were prominent in the students' reported notions of the Scholarship principle. Students rated highly the communication skills of academics. They found it important also for teachers to relate theory to practice both physically within the learning environments and to the real world of experience at work and other facets of life outside the university. Scholarship, as defined from the academic teacher perspective is (a) reflective, (b) inquisitorial, (c) responsive, and (d) communicative (Trigwell et al., 2000). Participants supported this notion, perceiving the Scholarship principle from a broader range of considerations that relate to how effectively they are assisted in their learning. Student responses indicated a preference for teachers demonstrating an understanding of how students learn. They appreciate it if teachers understand learning preferences and put strategies in place to accommodate individual differences in learning approaches, for example, to accommodate kinaesthetic, visual, and/or auditory learning preferences. There is sufficient evidence that students share the academics' views on scholarship with a varying priority given to their needs as learners (Trigwell et al., 2000).

The data has highlighted a practical and tangible student perspective on the nature of the Scholarship principle. Students' engagement in the discipline may have filtered the lens through which they viewed their experiences. They made limited reference to finer grained aspects of their subject disciplines and their teachers' engagement with principles of pedagogical content knowledge (see Schulman, 2004). Despite a concern that the definition put to students on the survey was narrow, they expressed a broad understanding. The definition "respecting diverse learning and teaching styles and upholding excellence and integrity of scholarship across USQ disciplines" elicited an understanding and expectation of quality teaching and learning that aligned well with the academic expression of scholarship. Central to the students' views of scholarship was how learning became manifest through the scholarly behaviour of their mentoring teachers. The notions of reflection, questioning, responsiveness, and communication highlighted by Trigwell et al. (2000) were evident in the students' understanding of the Scholarship principle. Students respected opportunities to reflect on their learning both within assessment items and beyond to longer term and wider application of understanding issues in their subject disciplines. Challenging matters raised within the academic disciplines through enquiry also reflect scholarly behaviour. An understanding is implicit that to challenge is a means of enhancing learning at the teaching-learning interface and it impacts on the integrity of communication for knowing. In seeking the students' voice, this data has revealed that students respect a pedagogy that embraces the Scholarship principle.

Flexibility Principle

In the student survey, the Flexibility principle was defined as follows: "USQ accepts individual and collective responsibility in providing supportive, inclusive and flexible learning environments." The data revealed that 63% of the 944 survey participants provided 568 exemplars (positive 73%, negative 27%). Relevant evaluations of the Flexibility principle were collated and categorised as follows. Following each category (in italics) student comments are provided. For identified instances:

1. *Teaching empathy*, including supporting student lifestyles; supportive teachers/lecturers who are inclusive, flexible, encouraging, and supportive.
2. *Constructive pedagogy,* such as providing meaningful and constructive feedback on assigned work, providing useful feedback and support with assignments, and providing clear learning objectives.
3. *Organisation,* in relation to lectures, online teaching, residential schools, workshops, face-to-face teaching, topic choices, open discussion, balanced tutorials and lectures, and provisions for self-pacing.
4. *Course materials*, for example, resources and teaching aids.
5. *Real life examples*, including applications to real-life situations.
6. *ICTs,* including multi-media use, chat sessions, study desk, online chats and breeze presentations, and other online courses.
7. *Flexible assessment,* for example, online submission and extensions.

8. *Other,* including rapport, consultation and research, and learning at one's own pace, but with support from teaching staff.

Responses from students who did not identify a course in which the Flexibility principle was evident focused on:

1. *No evidence of flexibility* in nominated courses; external courses not flexible enough.
2. *Lack of consistency* in between/among course leaders; ambiguous tasks and poor attitudes to students.
3. *ICTs not effective,* for example, technical support not good; Digital TV.
4. Other (not provided).

Positive and negative instances of the Flexibility principle are presented in Table 4.5.

Table 4.5: Positive and Negative Instances of Reporting Flexibility Principle Categories

Flexibility Category	Positive Instances	%	Flexibility Category	Negative Instances	%
1. Teaching empathy	58	14	1. Flexibility not evident	76	49
2. Pedagogy	131	32	2. Lack of consistency	42	27
3. Organisation	92	22	3. ICT not effective	5	3
4. Course materials	21	5	4. Other	31	20
5. Real life examples	12	3			
6. ICT	47	11			
7. Flexible assessment	23	6			
8. Other	30	7			
Instances	414		Instances	154	

Students reporting positive instances of the Flexibility principle commented favourably on their lecturers' empathy and understanding of life/work situations. This was further underlined by students citing instances of well-organised teaching practices with good use of ICTs, real-life learning applications and, when required, flexible assessment arrangements. However, 22% of all reported instances did not find that courses and/or lecturers were flexible to their needs, either with the use of ICTs or with inconsistency evident between staff members teaching courses.

Contextual Learning Principle

In the student survey, the Contextual Learning principle was defined as follows: "USQ recognises and values students' backgrounds and contexts." The use (or not) of the Contextual Learning principle within USQ courses was reported by 56% of the 944 respondents. Twenty-eight percent (28%) reported at least one positive instance of the Context principle while the same percentage (28%) reported at least one negative instance. Students' Contextual Learning principle evaluations were then placed in categories described below. For identified positive instances:

1. *Contextualised course materials* with identified links to life experiences, use of online discussions/forums/study desk, and collaboration inviting other people's stories.
2. Students' *beliefs and values* examined, showing an appreciation of others' circumstances, histories, beliefs and backgrounds; demonstrating supported and inclusive pedagogical practices.
3. *Work related* learning and experiences recognised in course materials; credits given for prior learning, relevance of course materials to work life; respect/empathy for workplace.
4. *Assessment* linked to work environment; assessment utilised work related skills and knowledge; and assessment provided opportunity to focus on individual interests and context.
5. *Teacher support* for contextualised learning, for the expression of multiple perspectives and values, for collaboration and sharing of ideas.
6. *Other:* A range of other responses which primarily included reference to gaining exemption /recognition of prior learning.
7. Context as it relates to *learning style* which accommodates individual strengths, circumstances, and requirements.

8. Understanding of students' *lifestyles and backgrounds* included in teaching perspectives.

Responses from students who could not identify at least one course in which context was evident were categorised as:
1. *Not evident*: No recognition of age or prior life experiences; no consideration for work or family commitments; materials did not relate to student context, living location/conditions.
2. *Not relevant*: Belief that student background or context was irrelevant to study.
3. *Other*: Study schedule difficult for international students, lecturer not clear, difficulty managing work and study.
4. *Cannot state, or remember*, any specific examples of Context in course.
5. *Too early* in student/s program to provide examples of Context principle.
6. *Uncertain*, but feel that Context may be included somewhere.
7. *No understanding* of what Context means.

Categorised positive and negative instances are presented in Table 4.6 below.

Table 4.6: Positive and Negative Instances of Reporting Contextual Learning Principle Categories

Context Category	Positive Instances	%	Context Category	Negative Instances	%
1. Course materials	66	27	1. Not evident	103	40.5
2. Beliefs and values	37	15	2. Not relevant	81	33
3. Work related	33	13	3. Other	30	12
4. Assessment	30	12	4. Cannot remember	18	7
5. Teacher support	29	11	5. Too early	8	3
6. Other	29	11	6. Uncertain	7	2.5
7. Learning style	17	6	7. Don't understand	6	2
8. Students' lifestyle	15	5			
Instances	256		Instances	253	

Findings from these data indicate that half of the students who commented provided positive evidence of the Contextual Learning principle in their courses. These students provided a variety of interpretations, qualities, and understandings of "context" inasmuch as they were able to examine their own positions, contexts, and values, to appreciate multiple perspectives and others' backgrounds and to link life experiences to the learning journey particularly through their own prior knowledge. Alternatively, half of the respondents were unable to identify a course that contributed to their understanding of the Contextual Learning principle–some suggested it was too early in their program and others not quite sure what was meant by the word "context". Others stated that they did not deem the inclusion of, or reference to, "context" as an important or necessary part of their learning journey. Chapter Five will explore Contextual Learning in more detail.

Discussion

The study's aim was to explore a representative group of USQ's students' views on the extent to which they believed that the five principles put forward to exemplify best practice learning and teaching at USQ were seen to be embedded within the pedagogical practices of those academics who taught into Semester 2 and 3 courses in 2007. Good to very good response rates for questions about the presence or absence of each of the five principles within their course/s for the surveyed teaching semester were observed for all teaching principles except the Contextual Learning principle. Instances as a whole were three to six times more likely to be positive than negative–the highest being for the Scholarship principle– except for the Contextual Learning principle where positive and negative instances were almost exactly the same. Additionally, the highest number of negative instances was provided for the Contextual Learning principle. These findings echo those observed for the Contextual Learning principle when quantitative survey data were analysed (see Chapter Three).

The qualitative analyses further indicate that the following aspects are important to the students' learning experiences: lecturers' attributes, such as positive interaction with other teachers and students; ability to empathise with students; strong academic skills and quality course materials and resources. Students were readily able to positively identify the presence of the Scholarship and Engagement principles, in particular. Indeed, the Scholarship principle was recognised strongly in the teaching processes, more than any other principle. This may have been because this principle has traditionally been an expected part of teaching in universities and therefore students could more readily identify its characteristics. Another rationale is that lecturers may provide stronger evidence of this Scholarship principle in their teaching than for the other principles. For example, the scholarship aspect of their work may emerge from their disciplinary expertise rather from their learning and teaching expertise. Negative evaluations mostly centred on lack of evidence for the principles in courses and lack of understanding of the meaning of the principle or the principle's relevance to their learning.

These results prompted the research team to think about professional development for staff based on the five principles. The team initiated a subsequent project to develop an online Self-Assessment of Learning and Teaching (SALT) questionnaire, designed to assist USQ academic staff to reflect on their learning and teaching capacities and to prioritise specific areas that needed development. SALT was designed to assist academics to develop their learning and teaching proficiencies by linking individual results to learning and teaching templates and exemplars already available on the University's learning and teaching support website. The SALT questionnaire was again based on the five "best practice" principles and informed from results of the student and staff surveys. Chapter Seven describes this third phase of the project.

Conclusion

This chapter analysed the qualitative data obtained in the student survey, and highlighted key aspects of students' perceptions of the five principles. For instance, in relation to the Sustainability principle, students considered that observed ethical standards in lecturers' teaching and professional practices and their strategic use of ethical and sustainable teaching materials–including real life teaching examples–were important ways for developing sustainable practices. The data also demonstrated though that students did not have a good understanding of that particular concept. Across the five principles, students' responses were three to six times more likely to be positive than negative, except for the Contextual Learning principle where positive and negative instances were almost exactly the same. The majority of positive student remarks emphasised teachers' attributes (i.e., professionalism; strong ethical principles, beliefs, and values; positive interaction or collaboration with other teachers and students; and empathy, support and understanding of students' work and life situations), teaching skills, and quality course organisation, materials, and resources. For a number of students, negative instances mirrored positive remarks insofar as these evaluations remarked on poor teaching skills, problems with course materials, and a general lack of understanding of students' needs.

Overall, the qualitative student survey data supported the importance and application of the five principles within USQ learning and teaching practices. The qualitative data reinforced the key findings evident in the quantitative data, highlighting the importance of the Scholarship, Engagement, and Flexibility principles, the problematic nature of the emerging Sustainability principle and the need to further investigate the application of the Contextual Learning principle which is expanded in Chapter Five.

References

Australian Council for Educational Research. (2008). *Australasian survey of student engagement. Australasia University executive summary report.* Retrieved from ACER website: http://www.acer.edu.au/auss

Coates, H. (2007). Engaging learners in higher and vocational education. *Research Developments, 18*(4). Retrieved from http://research.acer.edu.au/resdev/vol18/iss18/4.

Gosper, M., Green D., McNeill, M., Phillips, R., Preston, G., &Woo, K. (2008). *The impact of web-based lecture technologies on current and future practice in learning and teaching.* Australian Learning and Teaching Council, an initiative of the Australian Government Department of Education, Employment and Workplace Relations. Retrieved from http://www.cpd.mq.edu.au/teaching/wblt/overview.htm

Jashke, K. (2007). DEEDS: The 'Design Education Sustainability' Project, First Phase. *Research News, Edition 17.* Retrieved from University of Brighton website: http://artsresearch.brighton.ac.uk/news/deeds

Kennedy, M. M. (2006). Knowledge and vision in teaching. J*ournal of Teacher Education, 57(3),* 205. Retrieved from http://jte.sagepub.com/cgi/content/abstract/57/3/205

Kift, S. (2009). A transition pedagogy: The first year experience curriculum design symposium. *HERDSA News, 31*(1), 1-4.

Kuh, G., Gruce, T., Shoup, R., Kinzie, J., & Gonyea, R. (2008). Unmasking the effects of student engagement on first-year college grades and persistence. *The Journal of Higher Education, 79*(5), 540-563.

Pascarella, E., & Terenzini, P. (2005). *How college affects students: A third decade of research.* San Francisco: Jossey-Bass.

Radloff, A., & Coates, H. (2009). Doing more for learning: Enhancing engagement and outcomes. Australasian survey of student engagement

Australasian student engagement report (AUSSE): Australian Council for Educational Research (ACER). Retrieved from: http://www.acer.edu.au/documents/aussereports/AUSSE_Australasian-Student-Engagement-Report-ASER-2009.pdf

Shulman, L. S. (2004). New beginnings, old connections: Report of the president. *The Carnegie Foundation for the Advancement of Teaching.* Retrieved January from http://www.carnegiefoundation.org/about/index.asp?key=2227

Trigwell, K., Martin, E., Benjamin, J., & Prosser, M. (2000). Scholarship of teaching. *Higher Education Research & Development, 19*(2), 155-169.

CHAPTER FIVE

EMBRACING THE RICHNESS OF STUDENT CONTEXT IN PEDAGOGY

ALICE BROWN, ANN DASHWOOD, JILL LAWRENCE, AND LORELLE BURTON

Introduction

The learning environment of contemporary university students has undergone substantial change in an era of economic and technological change equivalent to no other period in history. The context for engagement with the academic discipline, the breadth and depth of pragmatic relevance to the professions, the physical global location of students, and the dynamic of learning and teaching are in a constant flux of change.

The demographics of adult learners in higher education have also changed dramatically, particularly over the last decade (Bradley, 2008). Students enrolled in universities come from knowledge and cultural backgrounds as diverse as their access to previous education and training. Bokor (2012) accounted some of the "drivers of change" to the dynamic industrial landscape that has led to the "democratisation of knowledge and access" and embraced "digital technologies", "global mobility" and an increase in "industry partnerships" (p. 6). Changes in the nature of universities and expansion of access to information has meant that locally, nationally, and internationally, students are participating in higher education from a diverse range of contexts (Organisation for Economic Co-operation and Development, 2011).

This chapter is the third of three chapters analysing student perceptions collected in the *Best Practice Learning and Teaching Survey* (see Chapters Three and Four). It specifically investigates the Contextual Learning principle. Contextual Learning, according to the transnational project (TP) team, refers to the importance of recognising and valuing students' backgrounds, and aims to ensure culturally relevant learning opportunities and assessment for students (Crowther et al., 2005). This chapter examines trends in higher education: an increasingly diverse student cohort in higher education; a range of interpretations of the term "context"; competition in the sector; and students' need for their contexts to be acknowledged and accommodated. A contextual learning pedagogy, as reflecting the extent to which current practices support a "strength based paradigm" where there is a mutual valuing and exchanging of ideas, celebrating diversity and life experiences, is also examined. The chapter concludes by making several recommendations for improving the quality of learning for an increasingly diverse student body. These involve constructing contextually inclusive learning environments and pedagogical approaches.

Theoretical Perspectives

Diversity in the Student Cohort

Over the last 20 years Australian universities have experienced a trend of double digit growth in higher education enrolments, with respect to both domestic and international students. Although factors such as changes to migration policy caused a brief decline to international students in 2009, Australia still ranks third behind the United States and the United Kingdom in tertiary international student enrolments (Australian Bureau of Statistics, 2011; Australian Department of Immigration and Citizenship, 2011; Organisation for Economic Co-operation and Development, 2012). As a cohort, those studying at university are increasingly diverse, comprising international, distance, female, and mature-age students that bring with them to the learning environment very different backgrounds, personal experiences, perceptions, and expectations of tertiary education, as well as unique engagement with course materials (Norton, 2012). Another significant feature of those attending higher education is the upward mobility of students from "socio-economically disadvantaged backgrounds and having parents with low levels of education" (Organisation for Economic Co-operation and Development 2012, p. 4).

Interpretations of Context

As noted in Chapter Two, many disciplines refer to context, and each has a slightly different interpretation. Reference to context often holds ambiguous meaning or is implicitly embedded, or alternatively it is specific to a given learning environment or situation (Oers, 1997). For example, McLaren and Hawe (2005) pointed out that in the field of linguistics, context refers to the text surrounding a word which allows a reader to gain a better understanding of what the word means. In art, "contextualism" refers to the way a work of art may only be understood by knowing the historical, political, or cultural circumstances during which it was produced (p. 7). Some interpretations of context are more pluralistic and acknowledge the process of "context making" or "meaning making" in a particular location or socio-cultural milieu (Dahlberg, Moss, & Pence, 1999; Shweder, 1990). Other definitions recognise context as one's interpretation of a situation or range of influencing factors, or as "a unique set of conditions or circumstances operating in the life of an individual, group, a situation, or event that gives meaning to its interpretation" (Brown, Dashwood, Lawrence, & Burton, 2010, pp. 37-38 ; see also Lawrence, 2006; Oers, 1997).

Competition in the Sector

In an increasingly diverse environment, tertiary institutions face new competition both domestically and internationally from private providers encroaching into the tertiary market, previously the domain of academe. The earlier dominant university discourse was challenged as student expectations and demands of their course enrolment increased (Bokor, 2012). Attracting and supporting students in terms of access, service, delivery, academic achievement, and quality learning and teaching have in turn become imperative for higher education institutions in terms not only of equity for students but also of the institution's sustainability (Commonwealth Government, 2009). In order for higher education institutions to respond to an increasingly diverse student cohort and meet the regulator's standards of ensuring they provide "a high quality education" (Tertiary Education Quality and Standard Agency, 2012), consistent evaluation has to occur in terms of the nature of study materials, university protocols, expectations for engagement, and the overall tertiary student experience (Arkoudis et al., 2010; Brown & Reushle, 2010; Commonwealth Government, 2009; Hannon & D'Netto, 2007). The ever changing context for learning requires a re-evaluation of the way courses and programs are offered. Modes of offer vary, and the range of full-time, part-time, online, blended and intensive programs are demanded by the education market, providing students with learning opportunities in an array of contexts and locations. Universities have also been forced to consider including a range of pedagogical strategies and processes that acknowledge the contexts and circumstances of all students.

Students' Need for their Contexts to be Acknowledged

Students currently seek equitable opportunities irrespective of their location, background, age, or lifestyle. Educators also recognise that for graduates to compete in a more culturally diverse world, students need a heightened appreciation of multiple perspectives (Bedford, 2008). As universities compete globally to attract students from increasingly diverse backgrounds, course teachers need to demonstrate pedagogical practices that recognise, celebrate, and build upon students' backgrounds, values, prior experiences, and contexts (Elson-Green, 2007). De Cicco and Kennedy (2012) and Frangenheim (2009) claimed that university teachers have no excuse, given the scope and advancements of digital futures and educational technologies available. With online delivery and the variety of resources available as well as an increased understanding of effective techniques to support the many preferred learning styles of students, equitable opportunities for all learners is the current reality for learning and teaching.

Providing a more seamless transition between personal and educational contexts through "contextualised pedagogy" in higher education institutions is not only an ethically responsible, but a necessary strategic and sustainable response to the new demands (Jones, Ladyshewsky, Oliver, Flavell, & Geoghegan, 2008). Student retention should be sustained and excellence in flexible learning and teaching standards attained as the Contextual Learning principle of pedagogy becomes the reality.

Towards a Contextualised Pedagogy

Context is interpreted vicariously in teaching as a means of maintaining student engagement in a course of study. One understanding includes the authentic listening and collective sharing of students' background, experience, culture, and stories as a means of valuing learners'' perspectives and linking their existing knowledge with propositional content knowledge of the course (Brown & Reushle, 2009; Oers, 1997; Singh & Shrestha, 2008; Taylor & Mulhall, 2001). Whereas past experience of university teaching might have been stereotyped as focussed on the academic imparting knowledge to those who chose to listen and follow, contemporary university teaching ignores the value of student context at the academic's peril. Brown and Reushle (2009) maintained that to ignore student context is to "teach with blinkers on" because it fails to consider the extent to which context impacts on student learning and the ability to learn.

In education, as noted in Chapter Two, pedagogical strategies include reference to terms such as "contextualised learning", "situated learning", "globalisation", "internationalising learning", and "transformative learning". These terms attempt to recognise the diversity and background of the learner and learning opportunities and assessment that support their context (Arkoudis, Baik, Marginson, & Cassidy, 2012; Burridge, Buchanan, & Chodkiewicz, 2009; Rutschow & Schneider, 2011). However, reference to context in higher education needs to affirm more than the importance of cultural influences and diversity. In many respects, context needs to be understood as being the "whole suitcase" that students carry with them to the learning experience.

Contextualised learning pedagogy celebrates the perspectives of students' "lived experience". This is a term that refers to an individual's idiosyncratic perspective, the unique set of life experiences and ways that, as individuals, students interpret experiences of what they know. Rather than a teacher treating all students as an "undifferentiated, homogenous mass" (Singh & Shrestha, 2008, p. 65) teachers find opportunities for two-way exchange of information and sharing of perspectives and personal stories. Supported by digital futures technology, such practices benefit from multiple modes of course delivery. Discussion on forum topics and live chat sessions facilitate collaboration of students with each other, with their teachers, and with a range of authentic environments established for the students to experience. These strategies provide a mechanism to help move learners into spaces where they can develop cultural literacy in a contemporary working environment and appreciate multiple perspectives (Elson-Green, 2007).

A key advantage in adopting a contextual learning approach is that students benefit from a double source of knowledge. They are enabled to move beyond their own values and belief systems to a more expansive cultural and contextual literacy (Hanne, 2010; Singh & Shrestha, 2008) and by extension, they learn to link the familiar to the unfamiliar (Ladson-Billings, 2001). Making connections enables students to draw on prior learning to help make sense of new information, as well as making the critical step to establish a connection between real and perceived borders of their learning journey and environment (Jasman, 2010). A contextualised learning pedagogy encourages students to make connections between new materials and concepts identifying relevance to their own context, situation, or life experiences (Aikenhead, Williams, & Hunter, 2000). Vygotsky (1978) suggested that contextualised learning is part of the scaffolding process. It supports students in constructing one-on-one learning experiences for one situation with a readiness to move on to the next. Such an approach recognises the importance of linking the life and work experiences and context of the learner to the learning journey while also ensuring that learning moves beyond a singular dominated perspective (Tarule, 1996; Taylor & Mulhall, 2001). Indeed, acknowledging context reinforces the "importance of the content of learning, as well as the nature of the learning situation" (Oers, 1997, p. 473). Research has shown that although international and overseas students appear to be satisfied with their "learning experience" in Australian universities, they also indicate a desire to engage more effectively with Australian students and educators (Australian Education International, 2007; Varghese & Brett, 2010). Contextualised learning pedagogy offers a collective approach for the sharing of intelligence between local and international students (Singh & Shrestha, 2008). It promotes appreciation of the complexity of global knowledge and the positive exchange of practices and beliefs. It also celebrates an open, inclusive, and borderless community of learners. The way tertiary educators do this varies according to their pedagogical beliefs, the course content, and learning outcomes.

Results and Discussion

Chapters Three and Four provide the research framework for the results that follow. Table 4.6 (Chapter Four) highlights categories of instances in which the Contextual Learning principle was identified as being evident in students' courses.

Negative Responses

A low 56% of the 944 student participants responded to indicate the presence or absence of the Contextual Learning principle within their courses. Interestingly, in responding to the question "Can you identify a course that contributes to your understanding of issues related to context?" positive and negative responses were evenly divided. The students described a variety of interpretations, qualities and understandings of context from their own positions, contexts and values in recognising multiple perspectives and others' backgrounds and to link life experiences to the learning journey particularly through their own prior knowledge. Of particular interest are the negative responses to the presence of the Contextual Learning principle in courses. Approximately half the respondents could not identify evidence of the Contextual Learning principle being present in any of their courses or they perceived context not to be relevant to their learning journey. The most frequent theme for negative responses (40.5%) related to students' inability to identify context- related information or themes being present in their courses.

Students elaborated the absence of the Contextual Learning principle in a range of ways. These included that their courses did not recognise age or prior life experiences, or had no consideration of work or family commitments, or that the course materials did not relate to students' living location and conditions. The following student quotes typify this first group of negative responses:

> "Apart from acknowledgement of prior learning to enrol in the program~ all materials so far do not consider any person's background."

> "...there was very little recognition of the knowledge and skills I had gained over the previous two decades."

> "Most courses are aimed straight down the middle of the class... If it doesn't suit you~ too bad. You're often told you need to decide whether you are a uni student or an employee!"

Another key theme in the negative responses was that 33% of the responses considered information on context not to be of value or not relevant to themselves or to the particular courses they were enrolled in. Students reported:

> "I don't expect a lecturer to always be able to take into account my own personal background and context. It's not really their job to do so."

> "I do not consider this to be a very relevant issue. The programs offered at USQ should be designed to prepare students for the workforce~ irrespective of background."

> "My particular background is fairly atypical~ so I learned early in my external studies that I could not expect that it would be considered."

Approximately 12% of the "other" negative responses were grouped together. These responses varied from international students raising points about their study schedule being difficult for them, to the lecturer not being clear, to difficulty managing work and study. The remaining 14.5% could not remember a course where context was clearly signposted or where they could identify context-related themes. Some suggested that it was too early in their program for them to respond in relation to this Contextual Learning principle. Others were uncertain or did not understand the question.

Positive Responses

By contrast, there were 256 instances reporting evidence of the Contextual Learning in courses. The most frequently identified positive theme (27% of responses) related to course materials that included consideration of context. Students cited cultural diversity and life experiences as examples of context considerations. For example:

> "....through using examples that you can relate to and know about and by not using USA examples that you know nothing about."

> "The course material for all three subjects included research/information about different cultures/contexts."

The roles of online learning and different types of collaboration were highlighted in considering context in courses. Students cited online discussions, forums, the course home page (StudyDesk) as well as collaboration with group work, and tutorials, as examples. They particularly valued collaboration with students from other contexts in forums and tutorials, and sharing other people's stories. For example:

> "We are given the opportunity in most subjects at one time or another to share past experiences."

> "Most courses do this by linking knowledge learnt in previous courses to the new content. They also always ask for our viewpoints."

> "The discussion forums provided an opportunity to discuss issues with students of other cultures who were prepared to be generous with examples of their life experiences that made the material that much more interesting."

This does not mean the courses always presented content in ways that fitted comfortably with a learner's existing frame of reference.

Students' Beliefs and Values

Catering for a diverse student population is still a major challenge for many tertiary educators (Reis & Kay, 2007). Context offers advantages for both students and educators. It encourages participants on learning journeys to not only have a reflective approach but to be appreciative of multiple perspectives (Brown et al., 2010; Oers, 1997). Students who completed the survey shared these perspectives on the Contextualised

Learning principle. They indicated that understanding context heightened their awareness of other possibilities outside their immediate point of reference and encouraged them to question their own personal beliefs. It also provided a richer, deeper connection to the course materials. For example:

> *"Part of the course is evaluating your own background/context~ which enables us to understand more about ourselves and others."*
>
> *"Learning about cross culture has helped to understand my own background and the background of other people in order to understand why people are different."*
>
> *"Within the learning structure of this course I have to investigate my own beliefs and discover the outcomes for assignments. Putting myself in others shoes to feel what they may feel within my scope of practice."*

Another common theme was acknowledgment and respect for other students' beliefs and values. Students highlighted that acknowledging others' circumstances, histories, beliefs, and values in teaching and learning practices was important in their learning. They also raised benefits of learning about other cultural values and seeing teachers embrace diversity and equity.

Work Related Contexts

Tertiary educators are now starting to appreciate the value students place on receiving materials in ways they see as relevant to their contexts and which acknowledge their prior knowledge and experience (Krizek, Birnbaum, & Levinson, 2004; Zepke, Leach, & Prebble, 2003). This form of contextualised learning integrates new learning with existing knowledge (Aikenhead et al., 2000). Boud and Walker (1998) commented that supporting contextualised learning means acknowledging that context "has a profound influence over who we are, what and how we think and what we regard as legitimate knowledge" (p. 5). Prioritising contextualising learning thus involves providing a culturally relevant pedagogy in which educators harness students' backgrounds, their prior work experience, culture, and history (Ladson-Billings, 2001; Reis & Kay, 2007). Current student data also recognised that learning encounters are effective when they capitalise on prior knowledge to connect to new content or skills. For example:

> *"I can relate the theory of my study to my current employment. This helps to cement my learning and give me a greater capacity for understanding what I am learning... also a greater motivation to learn too."*

Some students in this survey reinforced the benefit of contextualised learning by teachers valuing their work related experiences. Many responses made the connection of being able to apply relevant course work and materials in their work places. For example:

> *"Both educational subjects are enhancing and drawing on my previous experience working in adult education as a trainer."*

> *"I am currently working in Tax and found this course to be extremely relevant to my work and has helped me immensely. I use both my study guide and text books every day at work."*

> *"The course is relevant to my profession ~ and to the level that I have achieved in my role. I can use what I have been doing in the course today at work."*

Other students interpreted the inclusion of context in their course in the pragmatic sense of gaining credit in courses for prior learning and work. It was also important for a number of students that teachers demonstrate empathy and respect for the students' work and life experiences and commitments.

Assessment

Many students included assessment themes in their responses to the survey on the Contextual Learning principle, particularly with reference to work-related skills and knowledge. They acknowledged that assessment provides an opportunity to focus on individual interests and contexts. For example:

> *"The assignment was excellent and allowed for practical application of knowledge and experience I had before entering uni."*

> *"For the major project I was allowed to work in an area of interest and expertise meaning the project itself was relatively easy but the learning experience was far more valuable and I got more out of an easier assessment task that allowed for contextual learning."*

> *"I had assessment that involved students analysing their background and context and how it impacted on the way they communicate. And how that would impact on cross-cultural communication."*

Types of Support

A number of other positive context responses included teacher support, support of different learning styles and lifestyles. Students valued personal validation by teachers when they were encouraged to collaborate and share ideas with other students and with the teacher. Examples of students' responses included evidence of the educators' role:

> *"Awareness of students' individual requirements always portrayed....."*
>
> *"Aware of social strain and allowed flexibility in learning as dependent on individual needs of the students.*
>
> *"Taking into account the impact that background has on the understanding of students."*
>
> *"Considering everyone's background and context to achieve the best educational outcomes for all."*

In relation to supporting international students, Singh (2007, as cited in Elson-Green, 2007) suggested that one of the greatest challenges for educators is "finding a way to tap into that knowledge" (p. 1). For many educators, the difficulty comes from working out how to share the richness of multiple contexts with all stakeholders. Inherent in many writings and understandings of context is the necessity of collaboration as a positive means of acknowledging that learning is constituted in relationship with others. A strength of acknowledging the context of the learner in discussion forums is that all students can build community among themselves and achieve a deep connection with the course materials (Gay 2002). Shotter (1993) suggested that it is "the joint activity between [people] and their socially (and linguistically) constituted situation that 'structures' what they do or say, not wholly they themselves"(p. 8). In these instances an educator's role is one of facilitator and co-learner. Shaw (2009) referred to this "conscious use of 'difference'" or diversity as a valuable "curriculum resource" (p. 326).

In the qualitative results (see Chapter Four), the survey respondents referred to the Contextual Learning principle as it relates to their personal learning preferences. This was in relation to educators who accommodated students' individual learning styles, strengths, circumstances, and particular requirements. It also included examples where course materials were offered in a range of ways so students could use those that suited their preferred learning styles while still engaging with required course content. Examples of their comments included:

> *"It really suited my learning style."*
>
> *"By considering my disability and having to have time off ....my background has been considered when studying."*
>
> *"This course included lots of resources to access for different styles of learning."*

These findings are in line with a study by Boles, Hadgraft, and Howard (2009) which identified the value to both the educator and student of an awareness of learning styles. Understanding students' preferred learning styles helps educators to design course work and materials. Such findings are also consistent with Entwistle (2005) who commented that although there are a whole range of contributions that impact on quality learning and teaching, the consideration of student learning styles is worth pursuing. Student responses also highlighted that they valued examples in courses where educators showed an understanding of their lifestyles, backgrounds, and cultural issues. Comments included:

> *"My marketing lecturer was kind enough to allow me to email my materials in and gave me some amount of time to find my methods to send the hard copy somehow."*
>
> *"Anticipated arrangements have been made for me to do the examination using a computer~ taking into consideration of my osteoarthritic fingers."*
>
> *"As stated previously, knowing where an external student is living can help understand their lack of information due to internet problems~ Language problems and sometimes they face political problems."*

It is important to acknowledge the whole "suitcase" that students bring with them to the learning environment. The degree to which students can engage and make meaning from their study is dependent upon how well they make various connections. Context in this way becomes an intersection that links new learning with one's prior experiences, education, and knowledge. Therefore, a fundamental tenet of contextualised learning pedagogy should be embracing and using the "circumstances in which learning takes place" (Vosniadou, 1991, p. 283). This includes a symbiotic relationship between individuals and their cultural, political, historical, and social cultural milieu.

Conclusion

Inherent in discussion of the Contextual Learning principle is the necessity of collaboration. Leading educators now use a range of skills to develop multiple opportunities for students to interact, respond to key issues, and share their multiple perspectives, cultures, and contexts (Reushle, 2005). In the context of professional learning, Elbaz-Luwisch (2001) defined this as offering the potential for students to have "encounters with others who define themselves differently" (p. 86). This helps all students build community among themselves and achieve a deeper connection with the course materials (Gay, 2002). Shotter (1993) suggested that it is "the joint activity between [people] and their socially (and linguistically) constituted situation that 'structures' what they do or say, not wholly they themselves" (p. 8). Thus an educator's role is to encourage the group to collaborate while learning and engage with others to make sense of materials in their contexts (Cranton, 1997). In this way all learners benefit from a heightened awareness of both the similarities and uniqueness of others.

The findings gave credence to the notion that work-integrated learning should extend beyond students engaging in work experience. Smith et al. (2009, p. 23) argued that work-integrated learning is "an educational process, service, and experience, with foundational pedagogy and theory", highlighting that work-integrated learning "seeks to secure and maximise learning through experience, often outside the education's tradition". Work integrated learning is often subsumed under "an umbrella term for a range of approaches and strategies that integrate theory with the practice of work within a purposefully designed curriculum" (Patrick et al., 2008, p. iv). It is important that this curriculum is integrated and embedded into existing materials (Frawley & Litchfield 2009, p. 144). Moreland (2005) emphasised the importance of students learning about themselves in relation to the world of work and in turn developing greater personal and professional insights. Boud and Walker (1998) acknowledged the important influence of contextualised learning in understanding ourselves and our interactions with others. These considerations were also made when describing culturally relevant pedagogy, where educators harness a student's background, prior work experience, culture, and history (Ladson-Billings, 2001; Reis & Kay, 2007).

Work related or work integrated learning align with the Contextual Learning principle. Teachers, for example, need to consider and link existing knowledge with propositional knowledge. Educators might harness and build upon a student's background, prior work experience, culture and history, and embed these experiences into existing materials.

Higher education can achieve this by offering students a range of open-ended materials and processes encouraging them to connect the study materials to their own situations, and share details of their context with others. In this way, the course materials ensure relevancy and incorporate sustainable principles that demonstrate links between theory and real world applications (Lawrence, 2006; Rickford, 2005). This could mean offering a smorgasbord of resources from which students can select to help connect and engage with a course.

Although contextualised learning is still a major challenge for most tertiary educators (Reis & Kay, 2007), it has a range of advantages for both staff and students. One is that students benefit from "double knowing", where they move beyond their own values and beliefs and develop more extensive cultural and contextual literacies. From a student perspective, contextualised learning is valued because it enables them to link the familiar with the unfamiliar (Ladson-Billings, 2001). This is both in terms of drawing on their own prior learning to help make sense of new information, as well as helping to transition between real and perceived borders of their learning journey and environment (Jasman, 2010).

A growing body of industry and academic writing is now suggesting that effective learning and teaching needs to be contextualised (Han & Singh, 2007; Reis & Kay, 2007) to support students who are learning locally and others scattered globally in a range of diverse locations. It is important to consider ways to achieve the authentic listening of voices, acknowledge similarity and celebrate difference (Cook-Sather, 2006). The greatest challenge for educators is knowing how to enable students to tap into resources that maximise their potential for growth both as individuals and also as students engaged in learning journeys (Elson-Green, 2007). In this process, we hope to become familiar with our students' contexts, and ensure we recognise each student and do not merely treat them as part of an undifferentiated homogenous mass (Singh & Shrestha, 2008).

References

Aikenhead, M., Williams, C., & Hunter, D. (2000, April 14). *Teaching law to the nintendo generation.* Paper presented at the 15th BILETA Conference: Electronic datasets and access to legal information, University of Warwick, Coventry, England.

Arkoudis, S., Baik, C., Marginson, S., & Cassidy, E. (2012). *Internationalising the student experience in Australian tertiary education: Developing criteria and indicators.* Melbourne, Australia: The University of Melbourne, Centre for the Study of Higher Education.

Arkoudis, S., Yu, X., Baik, C., Borland, H., Chang, S., Lang, I., . . . Watty, K. (2010). *Finding Common Ground: Enhancing interaction between domestic and international students (A guide for academics)*. Melbourne, Victoria: ALTC.

Australian Bureau of Statistics. (2011). *Australian social trends December 2011: International students*. Vol Cat number 4102.0. Canberra, Australia. Retrieved from: http://www.ausstats.abs.gov.au/ausstats/subscriber.nsf/LookupAttach/4102.0Publication11.12.121/$File/41020_ASTDec2012.pdf

Australian Department of Immigration and Citizenship. (2011). *Student visa program trends 2004-05 to 2010-11:* Australian Department of Immigration and Citizenship. Canberra, Australia. Retrieved from: http://www.immi.gov.au/media/statistics/study/_pdf/student-visa-program-trends-2010-11.pdf

Australian Education International. (2007). *International student survey – Higher education summary report*, September. Retrieved from http://aei.gov.au/AEI/Shop/Products/Publications/Publication604

Bedford, L. (2008). Flexible grouping in the higher education learning environment. *Transformative dialogues: Teaching & Learning Journal, 1*(3), 1-9.

Boles, W., Hadgraft, R., & Howard, P. (2009). Exploring synergies between learning and teaching in engineering: A case study approach. *Australiasian Journal of Engineering Education, 19*(1), 19-26.

Bokor, J. (2012). *University of the future: A thousand years old industry on the cusp of profound change*. Australia: Ernst & Young Limited.

Boud, D., & Walker, D. (1998). Promoting reflection in professional courses: the challenge of context. *Studies in Higher Education, 23*(2), 191-206.

Bradley, D. (2008). *Review of Australian higher education - Final Report*. Canberra, Australia: Australian Government.

Brown, A., Dashwood, A., Lawrence, J., & Burton, L. (2010). 'Crossing over': Strategies for supporting the training and development of international teachers. *The International Journal of Learning, 17*(4), 321-334.

Brown, A., & Reushle, S. (2009). *The power of connection: Sharing epistemological approaches to reach beyond knowledge and skill acquisition in an Australian higher education context*. Paper presented at the 2nd International Problem Based Learning Symposium, Singapore (10-12 June), Republic Polytechnic, Singapore.

Brown, A., & Reushle, S. (2010). People, pedagogy and the power of connection. *Studies in Learning, Evaluation, Innovation and Development, 7*(3), 37-48.

Burridge, N., Buchanan, J., & Chodkiewicz, A. (2009). Dealing with difference: Building culturally responsive classrooms. *Cosmopolitan Civil Societies Journal, 1*(3), 68-83.

Commonwealth Government. (2009). *Transforming Australia's higher education system*. Retrieved from http://www.deewr.gov.au/Department/Publications/Documents/TransformingAusHigherED.pdf

Cook-Sather, A. (2006). Sound, Presence, and Power: Exploring 'Student Voice' in *Educational Research and Reform*.

Curriculum Inquiry, 36(4), 359-390.

Cranton, P. (1997). *Transformative Learning in Action: Insights from Practice*. San Francisco, CA: Jossey-Bass Summer.

Crowther, F., Behjat, N., Birch, D., Brodie, L., Burton, L., Connors, B., Cretchley, P., Dashwood, A.,

Hoey, A., Lawrence, J., Brown, A., Locke, J., Maroulis, J., Smith, A. and Wood, D. (2005).*Transnational pedagogy: A stimulus paper for consideration by the USQ professional community*. Unpublished manuscript, University of Southern Queensland, Toowoomba, Australia.

Dahlberg, G., Moss, P., & Pence, A. (1999). *Beyond quality in early childhood education and care: Postmodern perspectives*. Levittown, PA: Taylor and Francis.

De Cicco, E., & Kennedy, S. (2012). Learning in a digital age: Extending higher education opportunities for lifelong learning. Bristol, UK: JISC Innovation Group.

Elbaz-Luwisch, F. (2001). Personal story as passport: Storytelling in border pedagogy. *Teaching Education, 12*(1), 81-101.

Elson-Green, J. (2007). Looking beyond the western perspective. *Campus Review, 7*.

Entwistle, N. (2005). *Ways of thinking and ways of teaching across contrasting subject areas*. Paper presented at the Improving Student Learning Conference, London, 5-7, September. Retrieved from http://www.etl.tla.ed.ac.uk/docs/etlISL2005.pdf

Frangenheim, E. (2009). *Reflections on classroom thinking strategies* (9th ed.). United Kingdom: Sage Publishing.

Frawley, J., & Litchfield, A. (2009). *Engaging students and academics in work-ready learning contextualised for each profession in the curriculum*. Paper presented at the The Student Experience,

Proceedings of the 32nd HERDSA Annual Conference, Darwin, 6-9 July 2009.

Gay, G. (2002). Preparing for culturally responsive teaching. *Journal of Teacher Education, 53*(2), 106-116.

Han, J., & Singh, M. (2007). Getting world english speaking student teachers to the top of the Class: Making hope for ethno-cultural diversity in teacher education robust. *Asia-Pacific Journal of Teacher Education, 35*(3), 291-309.

Hanne, T. (2010). Caught in the Tower of Babel: University lecturers' experiences with internationalisation. *Language and Intercultural Communication, 10*(2), 137-149.

Hannon, J., & D'Netto, B. (2007). Cultural diversity online: Student engagement with learning technologies. *International Journal of Educational Management, 21*(5), 418-432.

Jasman, A. (2010). A teacher educator's professional learning journey and border pedagogy: A meta-analysis of five research projects. *Professional Development in Education, 36*(1-2), 307-323.

Jones, S., Ladyshewsky, R., Oliver, B., Flavell, H., & Geoghegan, I. (2008). *Academic leadership for course coordinators: Results of a professional development program pilot.* Paper presented at the Teaching and Learning Forum 30-31 January, 2008, Perth, Western Australia.

Krizek, K. J., Birnbaum, A. S., & Levinson, D. M. (2004). A schematic for focusing on youth in investigations of community design and physical activity. *American Journal of Health Promotion, 19*(1), 33-38.

Ladson-Billings, G. (2001). *Crossing Over to Canaan.* San Francisco: Jossey-Bass Inc.

Lawrence, J. (2006). *Engaging first year students: A collaborative approach implemented in a first year nursing course.* Paper presented at the 9th Pacific Rim Conference - First Year in Higher Education: Engaging Students, 12-14 July 2006, Gold Coast, Australia. Retrieved from http://eprints.usq.edu.au/archive/00000983/

McLaren, L., & Hawe, P. (2005). Ecological perspectives in health research. *Journal of Epidemiology and Community Health, 59*(1), 6-14.

Moreland, N. (2005). *Work-related learning in higher education.* Heslington, York: Higher Education Academy.

Norton, A. (2012). *Mapping Australian higher education.* Melbourne: Grattan Institute.

Oers, V. (1997). From context to contextualizing. *Learning and Instruction, 8*(6), 473-488.

Organisation for Economic Co-operation and Development. (2011). *Education at a glance 2011: Highlights*. Retrieved from: http://www.oecd.org/education/highereducationandadultlearning/4863 1550.pdf

—. (2012). *Education at a glance: OECD indicators 2012*. Retrieved from: http://www.oecd.org/edu/EAG%202012_e-book_EN_200912.pdf

Patrick, C., Peach, D., Pocknee, C., Webb, F., Fletcher, M., & Pretto, G. (2008). *The WIL (work-integrated learning) report: A national scoping study*. Brisbane, Queensland: Queensland University of Technology.

Reis, N., & Kay, S. (2007). Incorporating culturally relevant pedagogy into the teaching of science: The role of the principal. *Electronic Journal of Literacy Through Science, 6*(1), 54-57.

Reushle, S. (2005). *Inquiry into a transformative approach to professional development for online educators* (Unpublished doctoral dissertation). University of Southern Queensland, Toowoomba, Australia.

Rickford, A. (2005). Everything I needed to know about teaching I learned from my children: six deep teaching principles for today's reading teachers. *Reading improvement, Summer, 42*(2), 12-118.

Rutschow, W., & Schneider, E. (2011). Unlocking the gate: What we know about improving developmental education: MDRC, the National Center for Postsecondary Research (NCPR).

Shaw, J. (2009). The diversity paradox: does student diversity enhance or challenge excellence. *Journal of Further and Higher Education, 33*(4), 321-331.

Shotter, J. (1993). *Conversational realities. Constructing life through language*. London: Sage.

Shweder, R. A. (1990). Cultural psychology - what is it? In J. W. Stigler, R. A. Shweder & G. Herdt (Eds.), *Cultural psychology: Essays on comparative human development* (pp. 1-43). Cambridge, UK: Cambridge University Press.

Singh, M., & Shrestha, M. (2008). International pedagogical structures: Admittance into the community of scholars via double knowing. In M. Hellstén & A. Reid (Eds.), *Researching international pedagogies: Sustainable practice for teaching and learning in higher education* (pp. 65 - 82). Netherlands: Springer.

Smith, M., Brooks, S., Lichtenberg, A., McIlveen, P., Torjul, P., & Tyler, J. (2009). *Career development learning: Maximising the contributin of work-integrated learning to the student experience* (Australian

Learning and Teaching Council) Wollongong, Australia: University of Wollongong.

Tarule, J. M. (1996). Voices in dialogue: Collaborative ways of knowing. In N. Goldberger, J. Tarule, B. Clinchy & M. Belenky (Eds.), *Knowledge, difference and power* (pp. 274-304). New York: Basic Books.

Taylor, P., & Mulhall, A. (2001). Linking learning environments through agricultural experience: Enhancing the learning process in rural primary schools. *International Journal of Educational Development, 21*(2), 135-148.

Tertiary Education Quality and Standard Agency. (2012). *Higher education standards framework.* Retrieved from http://www.teqsa.gov.au/higher-education-standards-framework

Varghese, M., & Brett, K. (2010). I*nternational student barometer project 2010: National report.* Canberra, Australia: Australian Government Department of Education, Employment and Workplace Relations.

Vosniadou, S. (1991). Are we ready for a psychology of learning and culture. *Learning and Instruction, 1*(3), 283-287.

Vygotsky, L. (1978). Problems of method. In T. M. Cole (Ed.), *Mind in society* (pp. 52-75). Cambridge, MA: Harvard University Press.

Zepke, N., Leach, L., & Prebble, T. (2003, July 2003). *Student support and its impact on learning outcomes.* Paper presented at the HERDSA Conference, Christchurch, New Zealand.

CHAPTER SIX

EXPLORING THE FIVE KEY PRINCIPLES: STAFF PERSPECTIVES

ANN DASHWOOD, JILL LAWRENCE, ALICE BROWN AND LORELLE BURTON

Introduction

Chapter Six discusses both the quantitative and qualitative results for academic staff from the *Best Practice in Learning and Teaching* research project conducted at the University of Southern Queensland (USQ), a regional Australian university (see Chapter Two). Consistent with the student survey (see Chapters Three, Four, and Five), the quantitative section of the survey asked academics to rate all five teaching principles–Sustainability, Engagement, Scholarship, Flexibility, and Contextual Learning–on their importance in teaching, frequency of use, and use to extend knowledge. The staff survey also solicited participants' written responses about the effects of each of the five pedagogical principles on their teaching. Academics were then asked to provide written explanations for their *yes/no* choice to a question related to each principle.

Method

The academic staff sample comprised 54 participants ranging in age from 28 to 75 years old ($M = 50.2$, $SD = 9.6$). On average, participants had 20.5 years ($SD = 10.5$) experience in university teaching. All but one respondent spoke English at home and 22.2% of participants spoke a second language. The sample of respondents was spread over four teaching locations: Local Toowoomba (83.3%), Brisbane (9.3%), Regional Queensland (1.8%), and Coastal Queensland (5.6%).

Respondents completed the staff survey (see Chapter Three) and gave ratings on 19 questions asking about the five principles of teaching–

Sustainability (6 responses), Engagement (3 responses), Scholarship (4 responses), Flexibility (3 responses) and Contextual Learning (3 responses). A 5-point rating scale was used to gauge teacher perspectives on the five principles. For example, for the Sustainability principle, academics were asked to rate on a scale of 1 to 5, "How important is it that your teaching addresses current professional issues?"

The data was statistically analysed using IBM Statistical Packages for the Social Sciences (SPSS) version 20. The data was checked for anomalies and any missing data was coded prior to analysis. Following a simple descriptive analysis, ratings for the questions about each principle were grouped together to provide an overall mean for each principle.

Quantitative Results

Overall, respondents rated the five principles as being important in their teaching, used frequently in their teaching, and important in helping student learning. Figure 6.1 illustrates the overall means and standard deviations of each principle category. Additionally, the mode for every question on the survey was to the value of either a 4 or a 5. As shown in Figure 6.1, ratings were high across all principles, with the means ratings ranging between 3.9 and 4.5. The Engagement principle recorded the highest average ratings.

The three teaching application variables appeared to show differences. Paired t-test procedures were used to further explore the perceptions of the five principles. There were small, non-significant differences between *importance* and *frequency* for both Scholarship and Engagement. Significant differences were found between *importance* and *knowledge extension* for Scholarship, $t(52) = 5.10$, $p < .001$, and for Engagement, $t(53) = 2.36$, $p < .05$. These results indicate that although academics believed Scholarship and Engagement were important in their teaching and used frequently, they did not rate the use of these principles in helping student learning as highly. Academics perceived Flexibility similarly to Engagement and Scholarship. A small, non-significant difference was found between *importance* and *frequency* for Flexibility. A significant difference was found between *importance* and *knowledge extension* for Flexibility, $t(52) = 4.76$, $p < .001$. For Sustainability, significant differences were found between *importance* and *frequency*, $t(53) = 4.02$, $p < .001$, and between *importance* and *knowledge extension*, $t(53) = 8.23$, $p < .001$. This shows that although academics perceived Sustainability and Contextual Learning as important for teaching, it appears difficult to translate them into practice in a way that extends students' knowledge.

Exploring the Five Key Principles: Staff Perspectives

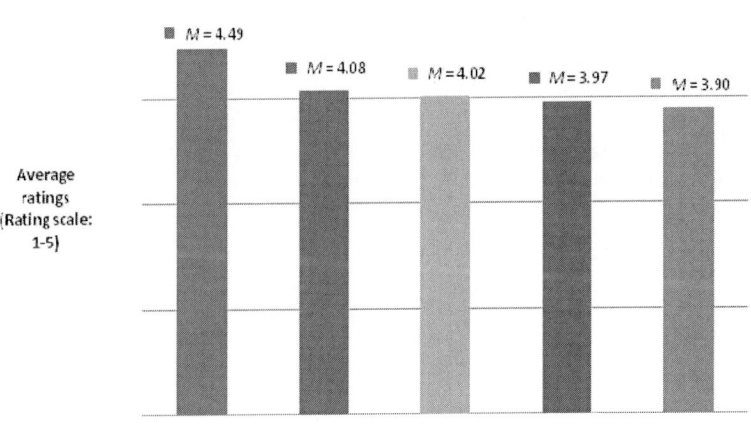

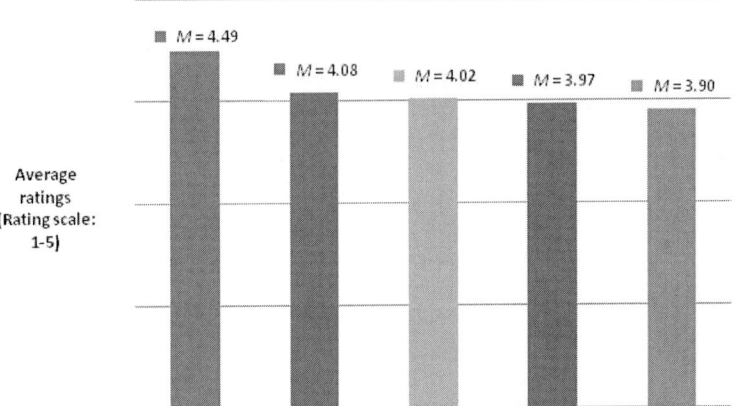

Figure 6.1: Academics' perspectives on the five principles

Overall, academics rated all five teaching principles highly on *importance* in teaching, *frequency* of use, and their use to *extend knowledge*. There were, however, notable differences within all principles between the three teaching application variables. Academics rated the perceived importance of each principle higher than both their perceived frequency of use and their perceived use to extend knowledge. This difference was significant in some cases. It is possible that academics attempting to apply these principles in practice encounter certain challenges and constraints that prevent this best practice teaching.

Qualitative Results

The staff survey also solicited written responses about the effects of each of the five pedagogical principles on their teaching. Following each principle's survey questions, academics were asked to provide written explanations for their *yes/no* choice to a question related to each principle. Consistent with the student survey, for the Sustainability principle, academics were asked, "Does reference to *ethical practice and sustainable futures* in your courses help students consider the impact of those issues on their professional practice?" Two open-ended requests followed - "If - yes, please explain how this was achieved"; "If no, please provide a comment." The qualitative data arising from these *yes/no* choice explanations were then collated and analysed.

The qualitative data from the 54 academics surveyed were collated into typed responses on Excel spread sheets. The researchers then identified themes, proposed category names, and reached consensus on titles for the coding. This method aimed to establish process-reliability, identify consistent coding, and eliminate duplication. Having established codes for the many response themes, each researcher coded the academics responses on the five principles to complete the full data set. NVivo software was used to collate those responses into the categories as binary qualitative data sets.

Sustainability Principle

The staff survey asked academics: "Does reference to ethical practice and sustainable futures in your courses help students consider the impact of those issues on their professional practice?" Overall, 94% of the 54 surveyed academics provided 78 exemplars (95% positive; 5% negative) of the Sustainability principle in courses. Comments relevant to

Sustainability were selected and categorised as follows. For identified positive instances:

1. *Ethics*: By developing credibility of profession/s; by maintaining professional standards; through use of case studies in ethical practice.
2. *Materials/resources*: Provision of resources and modules dedicated to sustainability in the environment and ethical practice.
3. *Real life examples*, including applications to real-life situations, providing an understanding of the global economy, impact on the lives of people.
4. Topics, projects concerning *future and current sustainable practices*, population change, scope for sustainable change.
5. *Relevant assessment,* for example, assignments, topics, projects referring to sustainability.
6. *Local and global issues* within teaching practices, including issues such as community development, business issues, and enhancement plans.
7. *Strategic teaching*, including discussions, case studies, authentic contexts relating to Sustainability, and teaching for life-long learning.
8. *Other*: General statements about the need for greater awareness of issues of sustainability, future learning needs, life-long learning needs, and ethical practice.

Categorised positive instances of the Sustainability principle are presented in Table 6.1.

Table 6.1: Positive Instances of Sustainability Principle Categories

Category	Positive Instances	%
1. Ethics	25	34
2. Materials/resources	18	23
3. Examples	8	11
4. Future	7	9.5
5. Assessment	6	8
6. Local and global	4	5.5
7. Strategic teaching	3	4
8. Other	3	4
Instances	74	

The four responses from academics that did not identify a course in which the Sustainability principle was evident were categorised as follows:

1. *Not relevant*: It was not a course role to provide sustainability; the issue was not particularly important; not of concern (for) learning; no need to contemplate the future requirements of course.
2. *Other:* For example, limited opportunity to address in the particular course taught.

Most academics considered that reference to ethical practice and sustainable futures in their courses helped students consider the impact of those issues on their professional practice. Only a small minority stated that they were irrelevant. Observed ethical standards in lecturers' teaching and professional practices and the strategic use of ethical and sustainable teaching materials were considered important ways to engage students. Almost 60% of positive instances fell into these key sustainability categories. Responses that provide examples of the Sustainability principle and capture respondents' views of *ethics* and *materials and resources* include:

> "Clinical Assessment and Intervention involves debate on ethical dilemmas... Ethics is covered in direct observation of client contact, case studies (and) obligatory familiarisation with APS Code of Conduct." [Ethics]

> "Talking about issues management and public relations practice where practitioners need to be advocates for the RIGHT activity or message as opposed to the LEGAL activity or message; doing the right thing... This comes up regularly and usually in response to an ethical dilemma in communication or discussion around the origin of spin." [Ethics]

> "... a considerable amount of learning material relating directly to the topics of acknowledgement of authorship and of career and study management are included. This material is intended to facilitate students' development of ethical practices in studying and learning." [Materials and resources]

> "..course content is geared towards thinking about these issues as they affect human security."

Unlike the student data, staff linked technological practices and sustainability. This reinforces Gosper et al. (2008) who found that reflecting about technological practices led to students' achieving better (i.e., more sustainable) results, and made it easier for them to learn. One participant stated that, for example, they included in their course:

> "...discussion about new technologies and the impact on future styles of production."

According to Welsh and Murray (2003), using critical pedagogy, a collaborative approach to innovation management (across disciplines and organisations), and a real-world context empowers students to use principles of sustainability to drive innovation in their discipline. Two of these three aspects were present in the data. For example, the use of critical pedagogy was frequently mentioned:

> "Preparing students to teach in a multiliterate world by using a socio-cultural approach to literacy and recognising that there are multiple literacies that occur within particular contexts."

> "In a course looking at understanding the development of students own prejudices and ways of becoming aware of those in order to overcome them when dealing with diverse clients.

> "The courses Introduction to Australian History and Race Relations in Australian History address the Eurocentric way in which Indigenous history was written and taught in the past and how Indigenous scholars have challenged the way both these fields are now taught."

This data also confirms literature in relation transformative learning (Thomas, 2009) and a value-driven approach to learning (Jashke, 2007) referred to in Chapter Two.

Participants also referred to real world contexts. For example:

> "My second year institutions and governance course referred to issue of global warming and we explored some strengths and weaknesses of the Kyoto~ international governance approach."

> "Sustainability~ in this context is whether we can continue our current practices of energy production and usage."

However participants did not highlight a collaborative approach across disciplines. In fact one staff member noted that teaching across disciplines prevented them from focussing more on sustainability:

> *"Note that my courses are required to support students across a range of disciplines~ hence we cannot focus on any one specific profession. This limits our scope substantially~ constraining us to generic needs."*

Themes in relation to inter-disciplinarity and collaborative learning are therefore emerging, which confirms the literature (see Moore, 2005). However, this staff member's equation of interdisciplinary with generic needs is not necessarily logical and could suggest that there is a need for professional development around interdisciplinary courses.

Engagement Principle

The staff survey asked academics: "Do activities designed to engage students contribute to their learning?" When asked to describe how the Engagement principle was achieved, 91% of all surveyed academics provided 78 instances (95% positive; 5% negative). Responses were categorised in the following ways. For identified positive instances:

1. *Strategic organisation* including tutorials, team based activities, problem-solving, critiques, small classes, residential schools, group work, and study groups.
2. *Use of information communication technologies (ICTs),* in particular WebCT, course home pages, StudyDesk, discussion boards, Knowledge Gardens, and blog posts.
3. *Interaction and collaboration*: For example, class discussions, open discussions: collaboration among both students and lecturers.
4. *Course materials and resources,* for example, course layouts and topics.
5. *Professionalism*: for example, well prepared tutors, weekly consultations (online), and supportive lecturers.
6. *Quality assessment processes*, including CMA tests, quizzes and projects.
7. *Personal interactions,* for example, relating to (students') own life situations; and reducing fears re study.
8. *Practicum,* such as clinical placements and class activities and practical activities.

Academics who responded negatively to whether they included activities designed to engage students in their courses nominated learning style and distance education teaching mode as reasons for their view.

Positive instances of the Engagement principle are presented in Table 6.2.

Table 6.2: Positive Instances of Reporting Engagement Principle Categories

Engagement Category	Positive Instances	%
1. Strategic organisation	24	32.5
2. Use of ICTs	11	15
3. Interaction and collaboration	8	11
4. Course materials and resources	7	9.5
5. Professionalism	7	9.5
6. Assessment	6	8
7. Personal	6	8
8. Practicum	3	4
9. Other	2	2.5
Total Instances	**74**	

A third of the academics (33%) who reported using the Engagement principle in their teaching perceived the ability to strategically organise tutorials, team based activities, problem-solving, critiques, small classes, residential schools, group work and study groups as most important in contributing to student learning. A third of the positive instances of the Engagement principle related to strategic organisation. Responses that provide examples of the Engagement principle, in terms of strategic organisation, include:

> *"Analysis of management of case studies by small and large group discussions~ individual & small group presentations of discussion findings to group."*

> *"... students work in groups and develop...a public relations campaign for an actual client. This then translates into higher marks in their next course...anecdotal evidence points to a massive improvement in marks for PRL3000 overall and a marked reduction in the number of failures."*

> *"My lectures are not lectures but huge tutorials where students are invited to speak and be recorded~ debate~ act in teams and take ownership of the presentation."*

In terms of coding, strategic organisation encompassed tutorials, team based activities, problem-solving, critiques, small classes, residential schools, group work, study groups, team work, forums, student PowerPoint presentations, workshops, telephone tutorials and class debates. The data suggest that staff perceived these activities and approaches as contributing to student engagement. These collaborative curriculum choices reflect the literature which maintains that an involving pedagogy engages students and is itself a critical feature of quality curriculum. For example, Pascarella and Terenzini (2005) recorded that:

> With striking consistency, studies show that innovative, active, collaborative, and constructivist instructional approaches shape learning more powerfully, in some forms by substantial margins, than do conventional lecture-discussion and text-based approaches. (p. 646)

It was clear that collaboration was a priority for some staff. For example:

> *"All work within the courses that I teach are structured around group participation and collaboration."*
>
> *"My course was rewritten with this in mind _ to focus students on activities rather than just a transmission/content heavy approach."*
> *"All of the project management courses require students to engage with their learning and assessment in the context of their workplace and work colleagues."*

A small number of academics (less than 5%) reported that student engagement activities that contribute to learning were not possible in their courses. For example:

> *"There are relatively few opportunities for students to engage in learning from a course offered only in distance education mode~ with a geographically dispersed student group~ and with very large enrolments!"*

This comment reveals at least one staff member's lack of awareness of the possibilities that new directions in online pedagogy provide (see Reushle, 2010). However, other data suggests that staff recognised ICT as contributing to engagement. The University is a multimodal institution with a large cohort of external/online students, so it is important that staff consider ways to engage students in all modes. WebCT, course home pages, the StudyDesk, discussion boards, Knowledge Gardens, blog posts and discussion forums were all perceived to contribute to engagement. Staff also gave examples of how they organised these to generate social connections and thus student engagement:

> "The discussion group is available to all students in each course, for example in group supervision and group clinical placement~ any student with resources/discoveries is encouraged to share with others."

> "Through participation in the discussion group~ providing scenarios based on the course content and having students make shared responses."

> "I ask students to get involved in the discussion board and provide interactive learning objects."

> "Students creating wiki pages with other students in the course; working with other students to prepare presentations using online tools students; presenting online presentations to their peers; using knowledge Garden.usq.edu.au as an optional student learning community."

Staff also perceived that interaction and collaboration played a role in developing student engagement. Participants cited class discussions, participation, face-to-face discussions, and helping others through activities like mentorships:

> "The majority of my law subjects have involved open discussion: collaboration among both students and lecturers; hands on learning, valuable facilitation, student-student dialogue, we discuss the theories and put it into real life situations."

> "My course in interpersonal communication incorporates weekly exercises and activities that have the students interacting with each other in applying and developing communication skills."

> "Professional mentorships and group presentations are vital."

> "I always use interaction activities during the teaching times to enable the students to apply what is being taught. I use games to engage them."

Some staff acknowledged, however, that interaction and collaboration are not always comfortable for some students:

> "Students have different learning styles. Some respond to more interaction than others."

The evidence confirms that effective curriculum design, in this case in relation to engagement, enacts an engaging and involving pedagogy. The Australasian Survey of Student Engagement (AUSSE; Australian Council for Educational Research, ACER, 2008), for example, provides clear guidance around the "activities and conditions likely to generate high quality learning" (ACER, 2008, p. vi) and reports that "all aspects of engagement have a strong positive relationship with a range of general, specific, social, personal, ethical and interpersonal capabilities" (ACER, 2008, p. ix).

Scholarship Principle

The staff survey asked academics: "Can you identify a course, learning activity, or assessment task that enhances students' opportunities to learn best?" With regards to the Scholarship principle, being identified (or not), 87% of the 54 academics described 69 instances (100% positive). The results were categorised as follows:

1. Belief that their *learning styles* were considered.
2. Appropriate *assessment*: diverse, oral, online-tasks.
3. *Organisation* of course delivery by means of residential schools, recorded lectures, oral assignments, case studies, hands-on activities and the study schedule.
4. *Quality teaching styles* that enhanced learning.
5. *Other*.
6. Selection of *real world exemplars* in the courses.
7. *Quality of course material* - how the resources and content were managed to make them accessible for learning and for assessment.
8. *Academic skills:* research skills development; focus activities, task-based ethics.
9. *Use of ICTs* in particular interactive software, online discussions.

Positive instances of the Scholarship principle were categorised and are presented in Table 6.3.

Table 6.3: Positive Instances of Reporting Scholarship Principle Categories

Scholarship Category	Positive Instances	%
1. Learning style	18	26
2. Assessment	15	22
3. Organisation	10	15
4. Teaching quality	7	10
5. Other	5	7
6. Examples	4	6
7. Materials	4	6
8. Academic skills	3	4
9. ICT	3	4
Total Instances	**69**	

Most participants identified at least one example of the Scholarship principle in their teaching. Learning style and assessment were reported as the main means of fostering scholarship. These two categories accounted for almost 50% of all reported instances of scholarship. Organisation and teaching quality together accounted for an additional 25% of instances reported. Responses that provide examples of the Scholarship principle and capture some of the views of academics surveyed under these key categories follow. In terms of learning style:

"On a given topic we provide tutorial activities for the kinaesthetic and extrovert learners~ model answers for the visual /read write learners and breeze slides for those who prefer to not attend lectures (as more introvert or auditory /visual learners) to assist students to learn."

"Students are asked to specifically identify own learning styles and devise specific learning activities using that style."

In relation to assessment, comments included:

"Having different types of assessment throughout the course... Not just write an essay!"

"My assessment tasks are scaffolded and specific resources are provided to walk students through the assessment required."

Academic staff perceived that assignments incorporating oral and online tasks contributed to scholarship. In some instances, computer managed assessments (CMAs) were used to help students to focus and keep on task. Academics aimed for diversity in the types of assessment, creating opportunities for students to prepare a proposal for each assignment, acknowledging their preferred conditions to undertake assessment and how it would be marked. Others provided scaffolding for tasks and specific resources in a sequenced organisation to enable variety and the staging of skills needed to complete the assessment items in class and/or on the web. One reported:

> *"Specific tasks are needed to push students beyond content knowledge to critical reflection."*

Academics further demonstrated that constructing assessment tasks was central to their scholarship, providing opportunities for students to critically connect to their disciplines.

Staff also nominated organisation as a theme. They perceived that connecting to the content and each other in a range of organised ways provides a framework for learning. Interactive discussion was valued as a means of connecting content and of connecting students with each other and the lecturer. For courses offered on-campus as well as by distance, a business lecturer's view of scholarship clearly indicates how important it is to make social connections between his students and their learning communities:

> *"Intensive mode courses are very interactive and provide opportunities for discussion with and between external students."*

Many others valued a "case study" approach and the practice of inviting speakers from the workplace and from industry into sessions. Where practicable, simulated settings substitute well for in-situ experience, particularly in project management and via clinical courses that explicitly apply theory to a task in a professional area. Teaching in a tutorial followed by strategic practice was a measure to staff of the effectiveness of their scholarship:

> *"Learning is a socio-cultural practice that requires students to be situated in particular contexts. Therefore the use of relevant authentic tasks is very important."*

Other traits in the data often subsume the quality of teaching. Lecturers need the confidence and social skills to create:

> *"Opportunities for students to approach a task in different ways."*

In order to develop such high level of skills, students have to demonstrate they are socially connected so that in a course, they might:

"Reflect and share their progress to learn by doing~ to collaborate."

Flexibility Principle

The staff survey asked academics: "Can you identify a course that helps your students learn by creating a supportive, inclusive, and flexible learning environment?" Responses saw 83% of the 54 survey participants provide 76 exemplars (92% positive, 8% negative). Relevant evaluations of the Flexibility principle were collated and categorised as follows. For positive identified instances:

1. *Teaching empathy/supporting student lifestyles*: Supportive teachers/lecturers who are inclusive, flexible, encouraging and supportive.
2. *Organisation*, in relation to lectures, online teaching, residential schools, workshops, face-to-face teaching, topic choices, open discussion, balanced tutorials and lectures, and provision for self-pacing.
3. *Flexible assessment*, for example, online submission and extensions.
4. *Constructive pedagogy*: Providing meaningful and constructive feedback on assigned work, useful feedback, support with assignments and clear objectives.
5. *ICTs,* including multi-media use, chat sessions, Study Desk, online chats and breeze presentations, online courses.
6. *Course materials,* for example, resources and teaching aids.
7. *Other*, including rapport, consultation and research, learning at own pace, but still have support from teaching staff.
8. *Real life examples,* including applications to real-life situations.

Positive instances of the Flexibility principle are presented in Table 6.4.

Table 6.4: Positive Instances of Reporting Flexibility Principle Categories

Flexibility Category	Positive Instances	%
1. Teaching empathy	14	20
2. Organisation	12	17
3. Assessment	12	17
4. Pedagogy	11	16
5. ICT	9	13
6. Course materials	7	10
7. Other	4	6
8. Examples	1	1
Instances	**70**	

Those who could not identify flexibility focused on the perception that it was not a major factor in determining how well students learn. Academics reporting positive instances drew on a wide range of elements that create a supportive, inclusive, and flexible learning environment for students. These included teaching empathy, organisation, assessment and pedagogy. A small number of academics viewed the Flexibility principle as unnecessary or not the major factor in determining how well students learn. Responses that provide both positive and negative examples of the Flexibility principle include:

> "Being responsive to their needs and being flexible." [Teaching empathy]

> "The teamwork works very well especially with my Asian students~ studying with USQ for the first time. It brings them into the project more actively and the team pressure ensures they do tasks and ask more questions." [Organisation]

> "Flexibility of assessment topics, moderate flexibility of study and assessment schedules." [Assessment]

> "Postgraduate students are expected to take responsibility for their learning and this is best facilitated by the lecturer encouraging open inquiry and challenge of didactic material." [Pedagogy]

> "...support & inclusivity is specifically addressed in external only courses through developing and maintaining an ongoing presence via study desk that is encouraging and informative~ aimed at giving the students a feeling

of having a home base for that course and a feeling that they are not alone in their studies of the material." [Technology]

"...I practise open door~ open email policies even with my big classes~ inviting direct correspondence~ answering even at weekends. And I support similar across my teams~ academics choosing the times and styles of communication they can and want to commit to flexibly~ rather than specific week hours. Staff flexibility is as vital as students~ and I think USQ forgets that in its attempts to regulate the teaching and assessment activities of academics. Some staff simply do some things better than others. The trick is to build well-balanced teaching teams~ rather than to create pressures and expectations of specific approaches~ no matter how valuable the latter are perceived to be. USQ needs to value flexibility and wide differences in academics too. That has declined badly in the last decade in an ill-guided search for a mould~ and even worse~ attempts to create such. [Inclusiveness]

One comment indicated the complexity involved in reflecting about the principle of Flexibility. A more negative reflection about the need to be flexible included:

"It is important for us to provide this (flexibility) as the students have a right to it but it is not the major factor determining how well students learn. Despite being a priority many other factors (some~ such as personal attitude~ largely outside our control) have more influence."

The varied nature of participants' perspectives on the Flexibility principle reflect an emerging literature about the range of rationales that underpin conceptions of flexible education, and the re-making of the official meaning of flexibility in national education policy (Palmer, 2011). Evans and Smith (2011, p. 1) argued that Australian experiences of flexibility have "created a foggy mélange: external studies, extension studies, off-campus studies, open campus, open learning, flexible learning, flexible delivery, distance learning, distance education, correspondence learning, online learning, e-learning, etc." Certainly, the USQ experience emulates this "fog" as it previously was known as a leading external and distance provider and its two latest strategic plans have prioritised online learning. Not that this research strand has marginalised flexibility as a concept or indeed a principle. Rather, according to Palmer (2011), the range of definitions has led to the point where flexibility might be found, or required, in nearly every aspect of Australian higher education. As a Deakin University Report (2009) argued:

...flexible education is complex, multidimensional and mostly includes the time and location of learning, the learning approach, the range of learning resources and delivery and is typically meant to empower the learner to select when, how and where to learn as suitable to that individual. (p. 5)

Contextual Learning Principle

The staff survey asked academics: "Can you identify a course in which acknowledging students' background and context helps them to learn?" The Contextual Learning principle's use (or not) was reported by 82% of the 54 survey respondents with 61 exemplars (97% positive, 1% negative) given. Academics' evaluations were then organised into the categories described below. The identified positive instances included:

1. Understanding of students' *lifestyles and backgrounds* included in teaching perspectives.
2. *Other*: A range of other responses which primarily included reference to gaining exemption or recognition of prior learning.
3. *Professionalism.*
4. Students' *beliefs and values* examined; appreciation of others' circumstances, histories, beliefs and background supported and included in pedagogical practices.
5. *Work related* learning and experiences recognised in course materials; credits given for prior learning, relevance of course materials to work life; respect/empathy for workplace.
6. *Assessment* linked to work environment; assessment utilised work related skills and knowledge, assessment provided opportunity to focus on individual interests and context.
7. Context as it relates to *learning style* which accommodates individual strengths, circumstances and particular requirements.
8. *Contextualised course materials* identified - that is, links to life experiences, use of online discussions/forums/StudyDesk, collaboration inviting other people's stories.

Negative responses were categorised as either *Not evi*dent–not a priority/difficult to address or as *Not relevan*t–belief that student background or context was irrelevant to study. Categorised positive instances of the Contextual Learning principle are presented in Table 6.5.

Table 6.5: Positive Instances of Reporting Contextual Learning Principle Categories

Contextual Learning Category	Positive Instances	%
1. Students' lifestyle	14	24
2. Other	11	19
3. Professionalism	9	15
4. Beliefs and values	6	10
5. Work related	6	10
6. Assessment	6	10
7. Learning style	4	7
8. Course materials	3	5
Instances	**256**	

Table 6.5 shows that academics provided positive examples of the Contextual Learning principle in a multitude of categories. Almost one quarter (25%) of positive instances related to students' lifestyles indicating they perceived this as a key area that can help student learning. A small percentage provided negative examples, stating that it was irrelevant as an aid for student learning. Responses that provide both positive and negative examples of context include those relating to an understanding of students' lifestyles and backgrounds. For example:

"Use a variety of examples to ensure that different cultural and gender groups can identify with the example."

"By allowing the student to choose the material to be studied- particularly if it relates to their background."

"Simple acceptance of background (mainly ethnic or nationality in practice and mainly applicable to on-campus students) helps them to trust me and be free to ask questions etc."

"My course encourages students to post discussion about their background and exposure to date to construction. This is to recognise that levels of exposure and understanding prior to the course are different and that all students have a valuable contribution to make to the subsequent group discussions and learning not matter their previous background. It is aimed at encouraging students who otherwise might feel disadvantaged in the subsequent discussions because they do not have an extensive background in the Australian experience of this course's topics."

"All Australian history courses are explicit about the biases of history. Students are asked to introduce themselves at the start of semester and international students are called on to compare and contrast particular Australian events with the experience in their country. But this is done at an informal level in tutorials only."

"In all my courses~ I start by surveying background and views about mathematics and learning. I can't think of a better place to start. And I believe that the resources and approaches I have developed out of this knowledge have helped my students learning. Certainly many of them enjoy my courses and do well."

Negative comments included:

"It is motivation and concrete learning assistance that helps students learn- not putting things into a cultural background. That makes it more fun for the students so that is why I do it..."

Contextualised learning and teaching appreciates the knowledge richness of diverse student cohorts, and acknowledges the importance of two-way communication, engagement, and collaboration between student-and-student and student-and-educator in the learning journey (Brown & Reushle, 2009). A critical aspect of support to students' learning and engagement is ensuring that materials are delivered in ways that students perceive as relevant to their context and which acknowledge their cultural attributes (Kuh, Nelson Laird, & Umbach, 2004, as cited in Brown & Reushle, 2009). Brown and Reushle (2009, p. 535) identified the following six learning and teaching conceptions as having relevance to both learning contexts:

1. Ensuring students feel connected, supported and valued as individuals and as part of a community of learners.
2. Ensuring teaching and learning activities have contextual application and relevance so that they are productive, meaningful and engaging.
3. Outlining clear expectations, approaches and levels of support to motivate and enhance the student learning journey.
4. Clearly communicating the pedagogical beliefs and approaches of the teacher.
5. Providing resources to suit a range of learning styles and to ensure maximum flexibility.
6. Encouraging and motivating students to embrace course content, concepts and the perspectives of others.

The review of data confirmed that these conceptions were present in staff and students' perspectives. That they are also concepts underlying student-centred approaches to teaching suggests that the limited research strand underpinning contextual learning can be widened to encompass literatures from other disciplines. These discipline strands are associated with student-centred learning (see Prosser & Trigwell, 1999) and social learning theory (see Lawrence, 2007; Van Dijk, 1997). In these literatures, human connection is seen as a fundamental ingredient in the teaching/learning process. From the sociological literature there are also Gee's (1999) ideas about diversity and discourses, or ways of knowing. Gee explained that each student can be perceived as a network of associations formed by his or her socio-cultural experiences. Appreciating the diversity of these "ways of knowing" in the classroom helps teachers to connect with students as well as acknowledge the cognitive, social, cultural, and political complexities the students bring with them into the teaching/learning process. As Gee argued, pedagogy with too narrow a spectrum of diversity is impoverished. As teachers, we need to make continual shifts in our teaching/learning practices to accommodate the diversity present in our classes. Chapters Seven and Eight will discuss in more detail the contributions of these literatures to the Contextual Learning principle.

Conclusion

This chapter explored staff perceptions of the five principles developed by the transnational project team (see Chapters Two and Three). Across the five principles, 82% (for Contextual Learning) to 94% (for Sustainability) of all surveyed academics provided statements about the presence, or absence, of the principle in question within their course/s for the surveyed teaching semester. Academics' responses on the teaching principles were mostly positive (96% of positive instances described). The highest number of positive instances (100% of positive instances described) were recorded for the Scholarship principle while the highest number of negative instances (1% of negative instances described) was provided for the Contextual Learning principle.

Most positive academic remarks emphasised the importance of including an ethical component in courses, as well as providing quality and engaging course materials, resources, and activities. This included the need to provide varied assessment tasks that cater to different learning styles and student contexts. Academics' remarks highlighted the need to support students' learning through empathy and by recognising and including different lifestyles and different learning styles. Providing meaningful and constructive feedback and support on assigned work was also a theme in many of the responses. Though the academics provided few negative instances across the five principles, those that were given provide further insight into best practice teaching. The remarks largely reflect the challenges and constraints academics face, perhaps most prominently those related to time restrictions and course delivery (e.g., large enrolment, external/distance education).

The staff survey data showed that consideration of the five principles assisted staff to reflect on curriculum design and delivery. Staff perceived that incorporating real world contexts and a critical pedagogy empowered students to reflect more about sustainability, as well as showing that social connectedness is a key ingredient in helping students engage with both the discipline and their learning community within the institution. Further, the data indicate that staff who perceived these principles as important considered them in curriculum design to enhance student outcomes. For example, staff who adapted course materials to accommodate diverse student learning styles perceived their students to be more connected to their discipline. Similarly, those educators who prioritised engagement in managing and delivering course materials engendered more positive learning outcomes for their students by assisting their feelings of social connectedness. Staff who drew on a wide range of elements to create a supportive, inclusive, and flexible learning environment for students also considered that these elements enhanced their students' learning capabilities. These included teaching empathy, organisation, assessment, and pedagogy. Staff also perceived that considering students' lifestyles was a key aspect of context that can support student learning.

The current data also indicate that in the higher education context, which experiences relentless change, the principles need to be constantly re-evaluated and refined. Chapter Seven will outline the development of an online self-assessment of learning and teaching (SALT) process to enhance teaching staff's learning and teaching capacities.

References

Australian Council for Educational Research. (2008). *Australasian survey of student engagement. Australasia University executive summary report.* Retrieved from ACER website: http://www.acer.edu.au/ausse

Brown, A. & Reushle, S. (2009). *The power of connection: Sharing epistemological approaches to reach beyond knowledge and skill acquisition in an Australian higher education context.* Chapter presented at the 2nd International Problem Based Learning Symposium, Singapore, Republic Polytechnic, Singapore.

Deakin University Report. (2009). *Perspectives on the future of flexible education*. Report prepared for the Institute of Teaching and Learning. Retrieved from http://deakin.edu.au/itl/assets/resources/persp-future-flexi-ed.pdf

Evans, T., & Smith, P. (2011). The fog of flexibility: The riskiness of flexible post-secondary education in Australia. In E. Burge, C. Gibson, & T. Gibson (Eds.), *Flexible pedagogy, flexible practice: Notes from the trenches of distance education* (pp. 231-242). Edmonton, Alb: Athabasca University Press.

Gee, J. P. (1999). *An introduction to discourse analysis: Theory and method.* London: Routledge.

Gosper, M., Green D., McNeill, M., Phillips, R., Preston, G., &Woo, K. (2008). *The impact of web-based lecture technologies on current and future practice in learning and teaching.* Australian Learning and Teaching Council, an initiative of the Australian Government Department of Education, Employment and Workplace Relations (DEEWR). Retrieved from http://www.cpd.mq.edu.au/teaching/wblt/overview.htm

Jashke, K. (2007). DEEDS: The 'design education sustainability' project, first phase. *Research News, Edition 17.* Retrieved from University of Brighton website: http://artsresearch.brighton.ac.uk/news/deeds

Lawrence, J. (2007). Two models for facilitating cross-cultural communication and engagement. *International Journal of Diversity in Organisations, Communities and Nations, 6(*6), 73-82. Retrieved from Common Ground Publishing website:
http://ijd.cgpublisher.com/product/pub.29/prod.423

Moore, J. (2005). Is higher education ready for transformative learning? A question explored in the study of sustainability. *Journal of Transformative Education, 3*, 76-91.

Palmer, S. (2011). The lived experience of flexible education: Theory, policy and practice. *Journal of University Teaching & Learning Practice, 8*(3), 1-16.

Prosser, M. & Trigwell, K. (1999). *Understanding learning and teaching: The experience in higher education.* London: SRHE and Open University Press.

Pascarella, E. T., & Terenzini, P. T. (2005). *How college affects students, Vol 2: A third decade of research.* San Francisco: Jossey-Bass.

Reushle, S. E. (2010). *Preparing for the future: Meeting the needs of tertiary education through the edgeless university.* ASCILITE conference, 5-8 December, 2010, Sydney.

Thomas, I. (2009). Critical thinking, transformative learning, sustainable education, and problem-based learning in universities. *Journal of Transformative Education, 7*(3), 245-264.

Van Dijk, T. A. (1997). *Discourse as social interaction.* London: Sage.

Welsh, M. A., & Murray, D. L. (2003). The ecollaborative: teaching sustainability through critical pedagogy. *Journal of Management Education, 27*(2), 220. Retrieved from: http://jme.sagepub.com/cgi/content/abstract/27/2/220

Chapter Seven

Learning from the SALT Fellowship Phase

Jill Lawrence, Ann Dashwood, Alice Brown and Lorelle Burton

Introduction

The transnational project (TP) team's journey to develop the meaning of learning and teaching at the University of Southern Queensland (USQ) started with the notion of "fellowship". A select team of academics (see Crowther et al. 2005) identified a transnational pedagogy based on five key principles (see Chapters One and Two). This was followed by research into the applicability of the five principles to both students and staff in the USQ context (Chapters Three, Four, Five, and Six). "Fellowship" then took on another meaning as the authors in 2010 received a USQ Fellowship grant to develop an online questionnaire–the Self-Assessment of Learning and Teaching (SALT) tool–with inbuilt sources of information and support. The SALT project was designed to comprise an online platform to facilitate capacity building among USQ academic staff, using the five principles as a framework. The platform would enable staff to reflect, prioritise, and develop their learning and teaching design and delivery capacities in line with the principles described in this book.

This chapter will explain the SALT fellowship project. It will outline how the project was conducted, including how the SALT platform was developed and piloted. The chapter will augment understandings already developed about the efficacy of two of the five pedagogical principles: Engagement and Scholarship. Chapter Eight will investigate the principles of Sustainability and Flexibility in some depth, cross referencing data obtained from both the staff survey (see Chapter Six) and the fellowship pilot. The Contextual Learning principle was specifically discussed in

Chapter Five, as perceptions about its meaning from both student and staff surveys were problematic. Chapter Nine will advance reasons for this by revisiting the literature encompassed by contextual learning.

The Fellowship

USQ Learning and Teaching Fellowships aim to "advance learning and teaching within the University by supporting leading staff to undertake high profile projects and activities that are of direct strategic benefit to the University" (USQ, 2012, p. 1). Fellows are expected to: undertake a project that explores and addresses an educational issue significant to the University; stimulate strategic change within the University; raise the profile of learning and teaching in higher education and the prestige associated with the pursuit of excellence in teaching at USQ; develop their personal skills and profile; and be ongoing advocates for excellence in learning and teaching at USQ (USQ, 2012).

Fellowship objectives

The research team secured a USQ Fellowship in 2010. Its primary aims were to develop an online self-assessment of learning and teaching (SALT) tool–comprising a self-report questionnaire–to: enable USQ academic to staff reflect on their learning and teaching capacities and assist them to prioritise areas for self-development; help staff develop their learning and teaching proficiencies by linking electronic individual results to templates and to exemplars already available on the University's Learning and Teaching Support's (LTS) website; and encourage staff to develop and apply an action plan as evidence of SALT completion. Figure 7.1 illustrates the processes involved.

Learning from the SALT Fellowship Phase

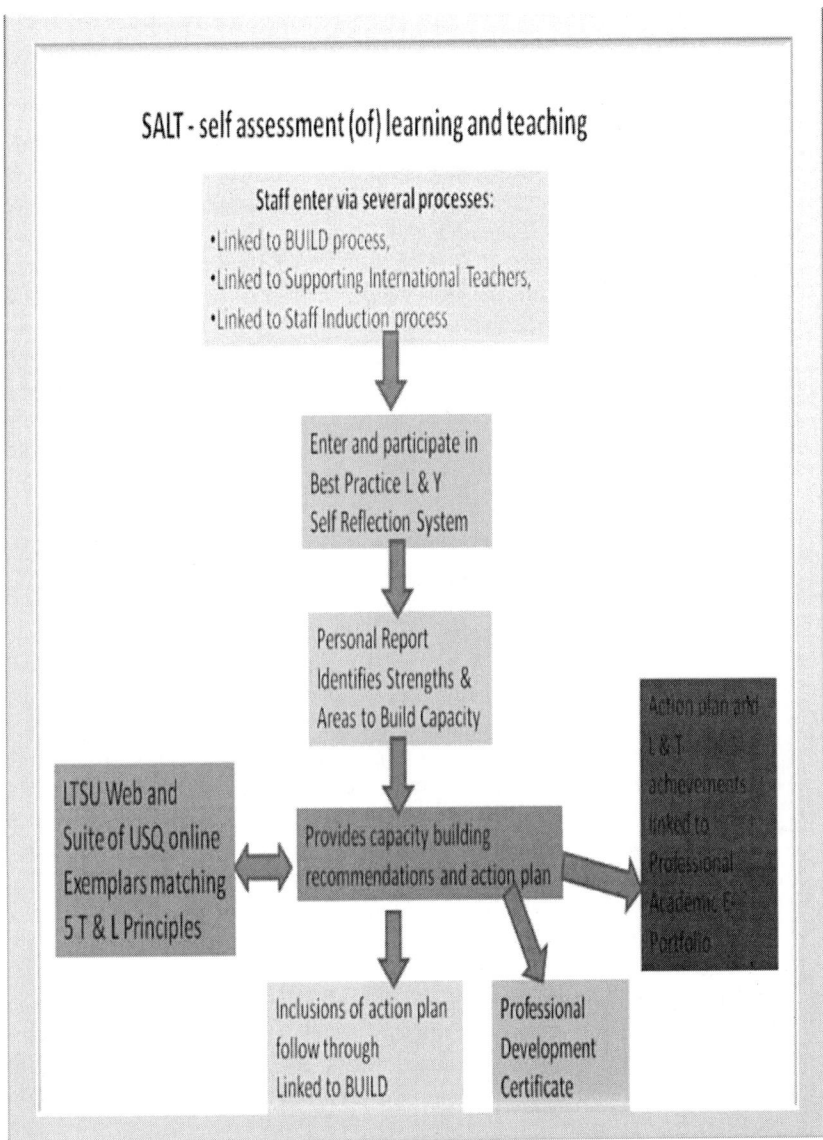

Figure 7.1: Map illustrating SALT fellowship processes

Secondary objectives were to seek feedback about the effectiveness of the SALT platform during and after its development. These included: consulting with stakeholders to evaluate the effectiveness of the questionnaire; liaising with relevant staff to integrate SALT into the "Building Upon Individual Learning and Development" (BUILD) academic performance review processes, and LTS professional development processes, such as embedding it within a module of the Graduate Certificate in Tertiary Teaching and Learning. The Pro Vice-Chancellor (PVC) Academic Quality, PVC Learning and Teaching, Associate Deans (Learning and Teaching), Associate Deans (Academic), LTS and Information and Communication Technology (ICT) developers were all consulted as part of this process. One further objective was to examine the effectiveness of SALT processes in enhancing academic staff members' professional development specific to learning and teaching. The research would include a qualitative compilation of views through focus groups to assess the effectiveness of the SALT design, including its framework for fleshing out the five principles.

Anticipated Student and Institutional Outcomes

The fellowship team anticipated that both students and USQ as a whole would benefit from the fellowship project. Anticipated outcomes included: facilitating more targeted support for academic staff; helping to improve the quality of teaching design and delivery; enhancing the student learning journey and student outcomes through staff self-reflection and BUILD processes; developing learning and teaching exemplars by aligning resources to the types of "best practice" support in demand; aligning with the strategic goals on the academic professional development of the 2009-2013 Learning and Teaching Plan (USQ, 2009b); and enhancing USQ's standing in the higher education community as facilitators of sustainable, equitable, and innovative teaching and learning practices across the institution.

The fellowship team believed that the SALT platform would assist educators to identify their strengths in pedagogy as well as areas where they might need support. Feedback from SALT would assist staff to critically reflect on their learning and teaching performance and develop new goals and objectives, assisted by the USQ links to exemplars and templates (see Brown, Dashwood, Lawrence, & Burton, 2010). The process aimed to maximise the potential for development tools to improve academic learning and teaching practices, and in turn, improve student transition, retention, and progression. A professional development process like SALT may also provide a way of embedding an institutional approach to learning and teaching.

Fellowship Processes

SALT was developed in four stages:

1. Identifying existing USQ online resources in quality teaching and learning to link prioritised areas to templates and exemplars available on the LTS website. Also, identifying other sources of assistance, such as LTS and faculty support.
2. Integrating a framework for a personalised learning and teaching action plan into the SALT platform. This would enable staff to develop a personal plan they could use as evidence in the USQ induction and performance review or BUILD processes, as well as in more formal qualifications such as the Graduate Certificate in Tertiary Teaching.
3. Piloting the SALT platform with selected staff members, and consulting with LTS and ICT developers on the questionnaire process and software.
4. Trialling the SALT platform with a group of international academics, on-campus and offshore, to fine-tune its use among USQ international academics and offshore partners.

The project was designed such that after participants completed the SALT questionnaire, they would receive feedback about their strengths and weaknesses (Brown et al., 2010). Another screen would prompt staff members to identify three key areas they wished to pursue and then be linked with a number of resources to help achieve their learning goals. These learning and teaching resources, most of which already existed on the USQ website, included exemplars and interviews with practitioners sharing ways to support student learning. Other resources included video clips demonstrating how to use various technological teaching applications and a range of recorded tutorials that support "English as second language" teachers. A print/email button enabled staff members to save a record as evidence of actions taken. A professional development certificate recognised actions and key areas of effort, and staff could link learning outcomes to their personal ePortfolios, which they could ultimately use in promotion processes.

SALT Platform Development

The SALT questionnaire was based on the five key principles–Sustainability, Engagement, Scholarship, Flexibility, and Contextual Learning–developed initially by the TP team (Crowther et al., 2005; see Chapter Two) and refined by our fellowship team. It was informed by data collected from USQ student and staff surveys of "best practice learning and teaching" (see Chapters Three, Four, Five, and Six). The SALT platform followed similar processes to those previously developed at USQ for the Academic Warning and Reflection Exercise (AWARE; see Taylor & Lawrence, 2007), an online self-reflection exercise integrated into USQ's conditional academic standing and show cause procedures. The SALT platform also collected demographic and evaluative data (learning analytics) from participants to investigate the efficacy of the self-reflection process.

Key stakeholders were consulted in developing SALT. The aim was to align teaching and learning goals with existing online USQ support features, ensuring equity and consistency in learning and teaching quality among staff at USQ and consistent with the current USQ learning and teaching plan. For example, LTS was developing eight modules of learning and teaching, with supporting resources of exemplary teaching linked to each module. The modules included: (a) assessment, designing, implementing, and managing; (b) materials, designing, developing, and being flexible; (c) strategies of teaching for enhancing learning; (d) curriculum design at program level; (e) technology for enhanced learning; (f) inclusivity for diversity; (g) evaluation of learning and teaching; and (h) excellence in teaching. The fellowship team felt that five key principles of pedagogy had a natural fit with these modules. Between December 2009 and March 2010, the team and LTS staff developed a matrix that cross-referenced the modules with the five principles (see Table 7.1).

The SALT questionnaire development extended from June through to November 2009. For each of the five key principles–Sustainability, Engagement, Scholarship, Flexibility, and Contextual Learning–participants were asked to respond to a range of statements ($n = 80$) using a 5-point Likert scale to indicate the extent to which the action was typical of their teaching practice. Appendix A provides example items in the SALT questionnaire.

Table 7.1: Sample Matrix for Curriculum Design Module

Module	Sustainability Principle	Context Principle	Engagement Principle	Flexibility Principle	Scholarship Principle
Curriculum design (program)	I enable my students to develop ethical practices for example relevant codes of practice I assist students to develop protocols of ethical practice such as appropriate referencing. I especially look for ways in which to build the concept of sustainability into my courses.	My courses help students understand their own values and beliefs in order to understand and hear others' voices. My students are required to reflect about and understand diversity.	I design my course materials in a way that helps them to focus their attention on the key learning objectives.	I structure my course by prioritising material for my students to access it as they need in a timely way. I design my course to promote students' ability to transfer skills and adapt to change.	New: I work with my program or discipline team to facilitate a whole of program approach to curriculum development. I am committed to a learner/student-focus in my curriculum design

Method

Participants

Two groups of participants were involved in the initial pilot to ascertain the effectiveness of the SALT questionnaire format and content. The first group were key stakeholders from across the USQ. The team used their networks to recruit the stakeholders. The stakeholders were staff from the five USQ faculties, and support services like LTS and the Student Management Division. Ten stakeholders participated in this preliminary stage. The second group were international academics who were recruited to not only investigate the effectiveness of the SALT questionnaire format and content, but also to discuss their understanding of the five principles and their relevance in learning and teaching practices.

Of nearly 600 academic staff employed at USQ, 101 are international academics–higher education teachers who were born overseas with their primary language other than English. The higher education context and pedagogy in those countries were specific to those cultures and languages. The fellowship team expected that working in Australia would require these academics to realign their past experience of pedagogical practice and teaching contexts with current expectations and strategic directions at USQ. This would involve adjusting language of instruction, cultural dichotomy, and epistemological and pedagogical difference. The pilot therefore aimed to extend the SALT process by developing equitable strategies to build the capacity of international staff teaching at USQ. International staff on-campus were invited in person and by letter to participate.

A total of 15 international staff participated in the pilot of SALT. The fellowship team targeted international staff as this was considered an area of need as well as providing an opportunity to apply an international lens to the SALT process. The sample comprised staff from Education, Sciences, Engineering and Surveying, Arts, Mathematics and Computing, Learning and Teaching Support, Business, Biology, and Physics disciplines. Participants were a mix of early career academics and experienced staff with time spent at USQ ranging from five months to 18 years. There were nine male staff and six female staff (see Brown et al., 2010).

Ethics was approved in 2010 and invitations sent to potential participants. The letters explained that the study set out to explore the development of an online platform for USQ academics to self-assess their learning and teaching practices, with a view to improving outcomes in pedagogy. It would primarily examine the participants' understanding of how the five principles related to their learning and teaching but also asked for their feedback about the questionnaire itself. A DVD of the SALT process was filmed and "Slip into SALT" (see mms://WinMedia.usq.edu.au/Temp/salt_web.wmv) was made available to orientate staff to the questionnaire.

Procedure

Two phases of data collection were involved in the pilot of SALT. In Phase One, the ten key USQ stakeholders were asked to complete the draft SALT questionnaire to ascertain its effectiveness in terms of format and content. The stakeholders were advised that SALT would likely become available for academic staff to use in self-assessing their current practices, and could constitute part of their learning and teaching portfolios. After they completed the SALT questionnaire they provided feedback about their experiences.

The 15 international academics also completed this stage. Participants were asked to complete the draft SALT questionnaire (60 minutes) and use the related resources (up to ten minutes). They were asked to submit a sample action plan. Confidentiality was maintained throughout and withdrawal of material assured at any time during the project, without penalty. Their perceptions about the items in the SALT questionnaire were collected to ensure that the items applied to their needs and were written in a clear and understandable way.

Phase Two, again conducted with the 15 international participants, included the collection of qualitative data using focus groups, comprising groups of 3-4 staff, and one-on-one semi-structured interviews with selected international staff. Participants were asked to discuss their understanding of the five principles and how they were embedded within the current learning and teaching practices and materials at USQ. The responses were analysed and key findings communicated to USQ staff participants via email and two campus-wide presentations.

The fellowship also set out to strengthen relationships with international staff by asking them to reflect on their learning and teaching using the statements in the questionnaire. In so doing, the fellowship team aimed to better understand international teachers' backgrounds and current teaching contexts. Further, plans were shared about the future development of the support systems and structures available through SALT. This process helped to assess whether equitable strategies were in place for USQ international staff to access knowledge of quality learning and teaching outcomes.

Results and Discussion: Phase One

After completing the draft SALT questionnaire, the stakeholders provided feedback about its format and content. Feedback included comments about questions:

> *"A few of the questions are still too vague; need more specific questions; reduce number of questions."*

> "Build in some 'padders' or some questions that are more easily attainable for the 'average' or even below 'average' staff member so that they will be able to engage with the questions and not say 'not achievable' for all of the them."

Stakeholders also suggested ways to generate effective resources:

> "For an online supporting resource such as the [learning and teaching] Modules, link questions to the resources so... if staff are unsure about a question make a link to one or two resources hyperlinked for further information ... or to the principle."

> "Look at chopping a series of video presentations to support international teachers. Using academic English effectively.... topic... have a simple Moodle course that academics can use... modelling types of language use... self-reflection activities... on using effective language."

Stakeholders further reflected on ways to increase staff up-take. For example:

> "Build in a certificate for actually participating in the questionnaire. They could use this process for a voluntary BUILD process and outline a plan of action on what an individual wishes to concentrate on."

International staff in the pilot also provided feedback on the questionnaire. This feedback emulated stakeholder feedback in relation to the questions. For example:

> "Break SALT into sections to reduce the length to allow time to reflect and respond."

Some comments referred to setting out, for example:

> "Add another column for ranking 'not applicable' where the question is not applicable to a course they are teaching.... Or 'if applicable'... 'where appropriate or relevant."

Participants also reflected about the resources provided:

> "It would be useful to have drop down boxes alongside items giving details and exemplars of good practice."

This feedback was valued by the fellowship team and the SALT questionnaire refined as a consequence.

Results and Discussion: Phase Two

SALT and Learning and Teaching

The feedback from the individual and focus group interviews with international academics showed that some participants had brought with them a range of strengths that paralleled USQ learning and teaching objectives. It was evident that for some international staff, the five principles naturally aligned with their personal teaching philosophies. Other staff had limited, if any, previous experience or knowledge about teaching in higher education. The assumption that international teachers have no prior experience in Australian and/or other Western style tertiary environments was challenged by the current findings. Contrary to expectations, the data showed that by the time many international staff are employed at USQ they often have two or three different types of tertiary teaching experiences either in Australia or in another Western university. This however, does not necessarily guarantee that they have experienced effective learning and teaching. One staff member expressed it this way:

> *"That was his philosophy... it came from his background. The average university experience in Indonesia is that it is more traditional and didactic."*

Participants also wanted more clarity on how SALT would be used as a self-audit tool. They had questions about its role in professional reflection; its potential for being mandatory for the performance management process at USQ (i.e., BUILD), or for learning and teaching development or research data on teaching and learning. They expressed anxiety about the exact purpose of SALT and voiced concerns about confidentiality and transparency. For example, one staff member testified:

> *"I have questions about the intention of the questionnaire linked to BUILD and will my identity be exposed."*

There was also feedback about whether SALT would jeopardise their need to gain student feedback. For example:

> *"I am concerned about student feedback and if I am working on some of these principles... it is hard from student feedback that they recognise or give us feedback on whether they can identify with improvements or see evidence of us using this approach etc."*

A number of benefits arose from the feedback, mainly around capacity building. First, the focus group sessions enabled participants to share their teaching and learning strengths, as well as the tensions they experienced in terms of pedagogical practice, values, and experience. Pedagogical conversations with peers about teaching and learning goals is an important strategy that any educational institution could adopt to heighten awareness of the difficulties international teachers experience in adapting to a different context (Boud & Lee, 2005; Parsons, 2010; Prebble et al., 2004). This would also help identify the types of additional induction materials and resources that new staff members require. At USQ, these could be included as support resources within the SALT platform. Providing this level of specific support would enable a smoother transition for all teachers, including international teachers, as well as clarifying real and perceived educational barriers (Dunn & Wallace, 2006; Leask, 2004; Smith, 2009). This strategy would help to minimise the degree of difference in a professional transition (Han & Singh, 2007; Jasman, 2010).

SALT and the Engagement and Scholarship Principles

First, for the Engagement principle, the SALT pilot showed that most participants recognised USQ had high level expectations about the benefits of student engagement. While an external motivator had encouraged some staff to think about student engagement, others had been intrinsically or internally motivated:

> "So we have to share everything with students. From this staff's background he worked in Indonesia with an American funding system and learned from the project to teach adults. His previous University presented prizes for the best lecturer and he got it twice."

> "The incentive of a prize had encouraged teachers to try to improve their teaching. Their other huge motivation however, is that these teachers get wonderful feedback from their students about the student's engagement. This teacher realised that the student's results/achievement were higher if there was engagement throughout the course. He was interested in building alignment and rapport with the student. And at the beginning of the semester he asked students to share a little bit of information about themselves and asked them the result they wish to aim for. This is kept by the teacher and when formative results come in they meet and they review and individualise their support."

> "Engagement is how to make students interact with each other and communication between teacher and the students....and then...the

activities should be more interesting. And encouraging students to continue community of practice and maintained and supported by lecturers."

However, in some contexts students did not want to facilitate engagement. In the Engineering and Surveying Faculty, for example, a staff member invited students to teach and talk to other peer students:

"And they refused it. Engineering students didn't want that...they absolutely refused it.......they said.... we are here to be taught...from PhD people."

The staff member reflected further that:

"What the students don't understand is that there are many ways to go about learning. There is not one method or one understanding....because engineers or students in any other discipline...if they can only operate in one mode (i.e., giving back what they are taught) they may not sustain their learning beyond their situation. As academics we have to understand that there are different learning styles....and be aware of the different learning styles and present this in a way to students...to say....there needs to be more than just reception."

The data further revealed that some disciplines were less likely to integrate student engagement in their teaching repertoire. One staff member considered that some members of a discipline taught in:

"An ivory tower and therefore in many ways don't feel they need to modify their teaching to support students. Students have to come to them, to meet the 'knowledgeable ones' from where they're at."

The same can be said about another staff member's experience in South Africa and the traditional approach taken in teaching there. Or the experience of another academic from Bangladesh who shared:

"He was very traditional in that he gives a lecture and then that is finished. There is no engagement. When he was a student he did not have any engagement ....there was a lecture and lecture notes and that was it."

This evidence supports Kuhn (1996) who reported that tensions often arise in relation to cultural specificity and cross-cultural interaction within the learning environment where one cultural practice may not transport across to another. Kuhn suggested that teachers may face obvious differences such as different learning and teaching practices, differences in institutional operations and role expectations, and even more implicit or subtle differences such as communication and engagement styles with students. In entering a Western higher education context, teachers may experience tension when they must "build rapport or connect with their students" through "chatting" or "encouraging students to challenge an opinion". Teachers who move from "high context" cultures may find that these practices and forms of communication conflict with their own pedagogical values, practices, and behaviours. Even a lecturer's teaching style or way of presenting can vary in terms of expectations and be a source of "mismatch" between them and their new place of employment. Leask (2004) explained this as a feeling of "teaching in a strange land" which then creates "an intellectual challenge and an emotional journey" (para. 6). The process requires teachers to adjust to the perceptions and expectations of both staff and students. It forces them to confront stereotypes, prejudices, and feelings of frustration and confusion. Smith (2009) shared an anecdote about an educator's experience of teaching in India where teaching is "religion" and where the profession is highly respected. In moving overseas into a new educational context the teacher realised that teaching was not as highly revered and students were not necessarily motivated to learn in the same way.

Some staff reflected that it was important to consider discipline knowledge when designing courses to engage students. For example:

"In engineering 'this glass tower phenomenon' may prohibit the ability to develop engagement because you don't present it or connect with your students at a grass roots level. It may not seem as worthwhile or important for course to be approached as funky and fun. The training/background in particular discipline, specialist in a discipline or in gaining a degree doesn't cover a qualification in pedagogy or an understanding of how people go about their learning or best ways of teaching."

Participants also reported that language and accents affected their engagement with students in a lecture or tutorial. Linguistic differences in pronunciation required adjustments from both the listener and speaker.

Overall, participants' evidence about the Engagement principle was twofold. On one hand, they acknowledged the tensions inherent in moving from one context to another. On the other hand, they were encouraged to learn about the practices they were confronted with in the new context and were willing to strive to enhance the engagement aspects of their learning and teaching practices.

Second, for the Scholarship principle, staff generally understood that scholarship involved their interactions with the new context and its learning and teaching expectations. However, some appreciated its nuances:

> "It is about the quality of how you understand learners and how they can learn and apply the information you are teaching."

Other participants expressed anxiety about not feeling adequately prepared for teaching and supporting students in the online environment. Even staff who had been at USQ for many years and had successfully mastered face-to-face teaching reported that they felt pressured and overwhelmed by the prospect of teaching online. Several staff suggested that they struggled with understanding how to best teach/deliver in an online environment and support external students. They suggested that this information should be used to orientate any new teacher at USQ, which is predominantly a distance and online institution.

Another concern participants reported involved online induction modules, which were implemented to introduce teachers to a range of teaching and learning approaches. On arrival, international teachers are included in an on-campus process, joining other new staff required to participate in the induction programs. These sessions are intended to induct all new academics into the University. They learn about human resources, new technology requirements, and the general running and policies of the institution. Online inductions followed these processes. However, participants reported that this was usually where the induction process ended for them. Most felt they were then left to their own devices to reframe and realign their pedagogical positions with the new contexts. Staff were also encouraged to enrol in the Graduate Certificate in Tertiary Teaching and Learning, designed to enable educators in the tertiary sector who already have a degree or diploma, to acquire credentials in tertiary learning and teaching (USQ, 2009a). However, the participants did not consider this was always feasible for a variety of reasons, including family and workload commitments.

The data confirmed that many participants felt the induction process and sourcing of exemplars was overwhelming and provided in an "ad-hoc" fashion. Staff tended to pick and choose from a smorgasbord of in-services or exemplars instead of working through them strategically to match their learning and teaching skills and needs to USQ's pedagogical expectations. They felt that the induction modules lacked depth, instead providing a more general understanding of learning and teaching benchmarks. Furthermore, these modules did not provide a thorough understanding of the context in which most staff teach, thereby failing to apply the basic principles of contextual learning.

Participants also identified a "pedagogical mismatch" or culture shock between past teaching contexts and the new institution's teaching and learning expectations and strategic directions (Hutchison & Bailey, 2006; Sarkodie-Mensah, 1991; Yook & Albert, 1999). These challenges are often compounded in tertiary institutions where teachers are expected to adjust their teaching approaches to suit the strategic directions, teaching and learning approaches, expectations and discourses advocated by their new professional learning environment. As one participant noted, their tensions were not only cultural but also professional:

> "These 'best practice' principles and policies touted by USQ may be in direct opposition to their philosophy of how to teach or believe teaching should be done for their profession. These principles may not sit comfortably with them not only culturally but also professionally."

Participants also felt they needed to adapt to institutional cultures and habits including "jargon, behavior, and norms of a new social group" other than their own (Packer & Goicoechea, 2000, p. 229).

The data therefore indicates that staff reflected about elements of the Scholarship principle as they adjusted to the USQ learning and teaching context. Their concerns emerged in particular as they confronted the pedagogical tensions that arose between their accepted ways of learning and teaching and the new flexible learning practices expected by USQ.

Conclusions

SALT

The fellowship project revealed that the SALT questionnaire needed major modifications before it could be institutionalised in USQ processes. Modifications included refining the number of questions, links to resources, and clarity of wording and layout. The pilot strongly confirmed the importance of making the purpose(s) of SALT explicit if it is implemented with staff. Other issues were SALT's inclusion in the BUILD process, and that international teachers would value ongoing focus groups or a community of practice which incorporated SALT. Further feedback was that USQ should include information on online pedagogy to orientate any new teachers. The pilot also suggested that there should be a greater understanding of international staffs' contexts and backgrounds and their impact on teaching and learning practices as well as a greater appreciation of how international academics can contribute to USQ's thinking about learning and teaching and students' needs.

A report written to acquit the SALT fellowship project included the following recommendations:

1. Following feedback and interviews with key stakeholders–including international teachers–a review and refinement of the SALT matrix can precede in the future (pending funding).
2. Online exemplars and resources of best practice require cataloguing, selecting, and linking to items on the SALT questionnaire to support reflective practice (pending funding).
3. Through pedagogical conversations detailed feedback was shared about learning and teaching experiences for international teachers at USQ. A community of practice would help to continue this dialogue.

Although the SALT fellowship project had finished, the pilot data indicate that more work needs to take place on refining the SALT platform and integrating it within institutional processes, such as induction and performance management, and professional development. Options about how staff will be asked to participate in the final version of SALT are also still being explored. For example, the SALT platform could be a valuable tool to integrate into educational programs such as the Graduate Certificate in Tertiary Teaching and Learning. This would enable a process of critical reflection on teaching practice, which would then lead to an action plan based on theory and the five pedagogical principles on which the SALT questionnaire is based.

Principles

The focus groups exploring international staffs' perceptions and experiences of two of the five principles revealed sometimes conflicting views. For example, while most participants recognised that USQ had high level expectations about the benefits of student engagement, other staff found that the students themselves were not interested in active class participation. Disciplinary contexts were thought to contribute to these differences. Participants did acknowledge the tensions inherent in moving from one context to another and the impact this had on student engagement. Some reported that they were encouraged to learn about the practices they confronted in the new USQ learning and teaching context while others felt more constrained in the new environment.

The participants also had firm views about the Scholarship principle. Some expressed anxiety about not feeling adequately prepared for teaching and supporting students in the online environment. Several staff suggested that they struggled with understanding how to best teach/deliver in an online environment. They were unsure how best to support external students and needed to develop their scholarship in the area. Some participants felt the online induction process and sourcing of exemplars was overwhelming and provided in an "ad-hoc" fashion. Others felt it important to socialise the five learning and teaching principles–Sustainability, Engagement, Scholarship, Flexibility, and Contextual Learning–among academic staff. Further work is needed to address these issues of concern.

A Final Note

This chapter has described the SALT fellowship project and extended the findings in relation to the Engagement and Scholarship principles. Chapter Eight will investigate the findings in relation to Sustainability and Flexibility principles. The final chapter, Chapter Nine, reflects on the journey undertaken by the research team. The journey is contextualised against both USQ and the Australian higher education imperatives to draw out threads related to the rapid changes impacting on higher education, in particular technological innovation and managerial governance. In doing so, the chapter investigates the applicability of the five principles in constituting the core of a whole-of-institution pedagogy: pedagogy able to retain its relevance and agile enough to respond to the rapid and complex shifts in the contemporary higher education environment.

References

Boud, D. J., & Lee, A. (2005). Peer learning' as pedagogic discourse for research education. *Studies in Higher* Education, *30*(5), 501-516. Retrieved from http://epress.lib.uts.edu.au/research/handle/10453/4924

Brown, A., Dashwood, A., Lawrence, J., & Burton, L. (2010). 'Crossing over': Strategies for supporting the training and development of international teachers. *The International Journal of Learning, 17*(4), 321-334.

Crowther, F., Behjat, N., Birch, D., Brodie, L., Burton, L., Connors, B., Cretchley, P., Dashwood, A., Hoey, A., Lawrence, J., Brown, A., Locke, J., Maroulis, J., Smith, A., &Wood, D. (2005). *Transnational pedagogy: A stimulus paper for consideration by the USQ professional community.* Unpublished manuscript, University of Southern Queensland, Toowoomba, Australia.

Dunn, L., & Wallace, M. (2006). Australian academics and transnational teaching: An exploratory study of their preparedness and experiences. *Higher Education Research and Development, 25*(4), 357-369.

Han, J., & Singh, M. (2007). World English Speaking student-teachers' experience of schools: Curriculum issues, trans-national mobility and the Bologna Process. *Transnational Curriculum Inquiry, 4*(1), 65-79.

Hutchison, C., & Bailey, M. (2006). Cross-cultural perceptions of assessment of selected international science teachers in American high schools. *Cultural Studies of Science Education, 1*(4), 607-829.

Jasman, A. (2010). *Future directions: Analysis of Australian initial teacher education policy initiatives.* Roundtable presentation at the Australian Teacher Education Association Conference, 4-7 July, 2010, Townsville, Australia.

Kuhn, E. (1996). Cross-cultural stumbling blocks for international teachers. *College Teaching, 44*(3), 96-99.

Leask, B. (2004). Transnational education and intercultural learning: Reconstructing the offshore teaching team to enhance internationalisation. *Australian Universities' Quality Agency (AUQA) Occasional Paper.* Melbourne, Australia: AUQA.

Packer, M., & Goicoechea, J. (2000). Sociocultural and constructivist theories of learning: Ontology, not just epistemology. *Education Psychologist, 35*(4), 227-241.

Parsons, C. (2010). U.S. students need to play catch-up, Obama says. *LA Times*. Retrieved from http://articles.latimes.com/2010/feb/23/nation/la-na-obama-education

Prebble, T., Hargreaves, H., Leach, L., Naidoo, K., Suddaby, G., & Zepoke, N. (2004). *The impact of student support services and academic development program on student outcomes in undergraduate tertiary study: A synthesis of the research.* Retrieved from http://www.educationcounts.govt.nz/publications/tertiary_education/5519

Sarkodie-Mensah, K. (1991). The international student as TA. *College Teaching, 39*(3), 115-116.

Smith, L. (2009). Sinking in the sand? Academic work in an offshore campus of an Australian university. *Higher Education Research & Development, 28*(5), 467-479

Taylor, J. A., & Lawrence, J. (2007). Making students AWARE: An online strategy for students given academic warning. *Studies in Learning, Evaluation, Innovation and* Development, *4*(2), 39-52.

University of Southern Queensland. (2009a). *Programs and courses.* Retrieved from http://www.usq.edu.au/handbook/current/edu/GCTT.html
—. (2009b). *Strategic plan 2009-2013: Creating sustainable futures....embracing the digital education revolution.* Retrieved from http://www.usq.edu.au/learnteach/qualpolplan/plans
—. (2012). *USQ Fellowships.* Retrieved from http://www.usq.edu.au/learnteach/path/grantsawards/ltgrantsfellow/usq fellows
Yook, E., & Albert, R. (1999). Perceptions of teaching assistants: The interrelatedness of intercultural training, cognition, and emotion. *Communication Education, 48*(1), 1-17.

Appendix A

Self-Assessment of Learning and Teaching (SALT) Questionnaire

Learning and Teaching Principles	Teaching and learning statements	Choose one that most suits your present actions or position				
		Never	Infrequently	Sometimes	Frequently	Always
Sustainability	In my learning and teaching research I model sustainable research practices such as consent forms.	O	O	O	O	O
	I integrate a range of learning strategies to enhance students' understanding of ethical dilemmas in my discipline.	O	O	O	O	O
	I incorporate a variety of learning and teaching strategies to raise students' awareness of the issue of sustainable practice.	O	O	O	O	O
Engagement	I use class discussion and participation to enhance student engagement.	O	O	O	O	O
	I use problem solving techniques to help students engage with the content.	O	O	O	O	O
	I use group work to facilitate engagement.	O	O	O	O	O
	I am well prepared for my lectures/tutorials/and consultations online and face-to-face to help students' access relevant materials and to communicate effectively.	O	O	O	O	O
	I recognise that student engagement is a two-way and reciprocal process.	O	O	O	O	O
Flexibility	I accommodate for the specific learning needs of students with disabilities or illness.	O	O	O	O	O

	I support flexible learning principles by ensuring that I am available for student consultation and observe at least minimum USQ standards.	O	O	O	O	O
	I organise discussion groups/ group design to facilitate peer review, communication and self-directed learning.	O	O	O	O	O
	I use Peer review activities to enable students to self monitor their learning.	O	O	O	O	O
Context	My students are encouraged to share their personal and work experiences relevant to the topic and discipline.	O	O	O	O	O
	I use a variety of examples to ensure that different cultural and gender groups can identify with an example.	O	O	O	O	O
	I use strategies enabling students to relate concepts to their personal contexts promote a safe learning environment in which they can ask questions.	O	O	O	O	O
	I help students develop learning strategies.	O	O	O	O	O
	I am aware that students' cultural backgrounds affect their approaches to learning student and develop strategies to help them adjust.	O	O	O	O	O
Scholar-ship	I organise opportunities for my students to participate in active learning (e.g., tutorials, online discussion, and/or residential college).	O	O	O	O	O
	I build in teamwork activities so that students learn to build on each other's strengths.	O	O	O	O	O
	I integrate my personal and professional experiences to help students connect to the discipline;	O	O	O	O	O
	I am organised, explicit and clear in my teaching approach.	O	O	O	O	O
	I make my learning expectations explicit to students.	O	O	O	O	O

CHAPTER EIGHT

UNRAVELLING THE MEANING
OF SUSTAINABILITY AND FLEXIBILITY
FOR A PEDAGOGY

ANN DASHWOOD, ALICE BROWN,
JILL LAWRENCE AND LORELLE BURTON

Introduction

Understandings of the terms Sustainability and Flexibility abound as they have evolved to become bi-directional words in contemporary education. These two principles of higher education pedagogy were introduced in Chapter One and their meanings elaborated upon in Chapter Two. Chapters Three and Four enriched those definitions, discussing students' perceptions of how the two principles were integrated into their courses. Chapter Six outlined insights by academic staff and Chapter Seven described the Self-Assessment of Learning and Teaching (SALT) fellowship phase. This chapter will revisit academics' perceptions revealed in the staff survey and review data generated in the SALT fellowship project, scrutinising the dichotomy of meanings attributed to Sustainability and Flexibility from strategic intent to grassroots application.

In this chapter, we specifically interpret academics' understandings of two key principles, Sustainability and Flexibility. Academics' responses to the staff survey (Chapter Four) and focus group data from a sample of on-campus international academics (see Chapter Seven) were used to inform the current analysis of these two principles. The chapter concludes by proposing strategies for consistent, ethical and sustainable pedagogies that would align flexible teaching approaches with strategic directions for contemporary university pedagogy.

Positioning Principles of Pedagogy

Higher education institutions make strategic plans for learning and teaching. Within those plans are the organisation's key intentions, which are integral in promoting the university as a learning institution. But in the process of accessing, interpreting, and passing on concepts to others, key messages in the guiding pedagogical principles can become lost in translation, leaving staff with multiple understandings of the concepts in practice (Djordjevic & Cotton, 2011). Ambiguity and mixed interpretations may occur as information filters from the corporate vision to grassroots stakeholders with the effect of polarising the corporate vision and individual members' perspectives.

Both Sustainability and Flexibility are concepts currently referred to in the University of Southern Queensland's (USQ, 2011) strategic plan. In the following sections, we revisit the Sustainability and Flexibility principles, positioning them against strategic directions generated by universities in response to global, national, and local forces of change.

Sustainability Principle

Use of the term "sustainability" in higher education is now widespread although its meaning is not consistently applied. The theme has become a key developmental agenda item for more than 600 universities worldwide (Leal Filho, 2000). While universities have committed themselves to the sustainability concept through various declarations and charters (e.g., the Halifax Declaration, the Bologna Charter, the 2010 Campus Sustainability Review, and the Australasian Campuses towards Sustainability Network) an agreed interpretation of sustainability remains elusive (Kennedy, 2006).

The "sustainability" term came into popular parlance in the late 1970s, aligned directly with resource efficiency and the systematic, long-term use of natural resources, particularly forestry resources. It has now evolved for multiple uses within the higher education sector with misconceptions (Leal Filho, 2000) having a negative impact on the ability of an organisation to implement sustainability into pedagogy. The United National Educational Scientific and Cultural Organisation (UNESCO) world conference on education for sustainable development encompassed broad parameters for promoting quality education inclusive of all people based on values, principles, and practices necessary to respond effectively to current and future challenges. Education for sustainable development emphasised "creative and critical approaches, long-term thinking, innovation and empowerment for dealing with uncertainty, and for solving complex problems" Bonn Declaration, (2009, pp. 1-2). Sustainability emphasises creative and critical approaches, long-term thinking, innovation, and empowerment for dealing with uncertainty, and solving complex problems.

Currently, international journals, reports, policy documents, national networks and institutions adopt sustainable principles in three main areas: sustainable organisational strategies and approaches, focused on the long term viability of an organisation (see Scott, Coates, and Anderson, 2008); ecological models of sustainable environmental approaches adopted at an institutional level, related to "environmentally friendly", "green campuses" and "green team" initiatives (Sharp, 2002); and pedagogical "real world" sustainability, in discussions in teaching and learning and curriculum development. The latter focusing on sustainable future-related links between what is taught and how this flows into the workforce now and in the future (Foster, 2002; Gosper et al., 2008). The term "sustainable futures", as discussed in Chapter Two has expanded into learning and teaching to encompass its interdisciplinary nature, critical thinking (Thomas, 2009), transformative learning (Moore, 2005) and lifelong learning (Jashke, 2007). There are also institutional views of sustainable practice which involve "a process of learning how to make decisions that consider the long-term future of the economy, ecology and equity of all communities" (Djordjevic & Cotton, 2011, p. 381). This expands on Sterling's (2004) view that the more inclusive the definition, the higher the potential of being a "gateway to a different view of curriculum, of pedagogy, of organizational change, of policy and particularly of ethos" (p. 50).

Strategic Directions in *Sustainability*

Institutions of higher education in Europe have already recognised that preparation is required in order to pursue sustainability at the practical level of management as well as teaching. Establishing in-service training and working groups to pursue initiatives, developing networks within the university and across universities to exchange ideas and experiences, and establishing a timetable and overall action plan are integral (Leal Filho, 2000). In the Australian context, tertiary institutions have developed statements of purpose that reflect their core values in terms of how they aim to support a "world class" higher education opportunity. Marketing strategies also align with strategic directions and core statements by articulating the distinguishing factors. Those statements embed principles that reinforce the aspirations of the institution. For instance, University of Melbourne's "triple helix" metaphor is used to describe three interconnecting strands of core activities–research, learning and teaching, and engagement–which together define the direction and intentions of the university (Growing Esteem, 2010). Nine principles of teaching and learning guide the pedagogy adopted by the university.

In a climate of increasing accountability, competitiveness, and awareness of pedagogically informed teaching and learning principles, higher education institutions are embedding guiding statements into their operations, strategic plans, directions, and organisational vision. Most Australian universities implement graduate qualities or skills that students need to develop to be successful in their future careers. If these are mapped and aligned through programs/courses or degrees they could constitute a unifying pedagogical practice, though there is limited theory to flesh out the rationale for unifying the qualities in this way. The Federal Australian Government has also mandated a quality agency to ensure that universities are accountable for standards and quality assurance arrangements. Each university now enters into a formal compact with the government around their levels of service. In 2011, the Tertiary Education Quality and Standards Agency (TEQSA) was established to build on the strong efforts of the Australian Universities Quality Agency (AUQA) that was previously in place.

The vision and mission of USQ (2011) is to be accessible, flexible, and borderless and provide fulfilling experiences for all students. Its vision expands to include being a world leader in open and flexible higher education, developing graduates for sustainable futures ready to engage with communities, business and government through ongoing and mutually beneficial partnerships (USQ, 2010; 2011). USQ uses benchmarking–a "strategic and systematic learning approach of continuous comparative and evaluation processes against organisations, both national and international" (USQ, n.d, p. 7) –to monitor its effectiveness in meeting quality standards of the higher education sector. According to the Australasian Council on Open Distance and E-Learning (ACODE, 2008), benchmarks relate to institution policy and governance for technology supported learning and teaching. They also pertain to quality improvement of the integration of technologies for learning and teaching, information technology infrastructure to support learning and teaching, and pedagogical application of information and communication technology. Additionally, professional/staff development for the effective use of technologies for learning and teaching, and student and staff support for the effective use of technologies for learning and teaching, are covered in these benchmarks.

During the period 2009-2013, USQ took a "cascading" approach to the process of promoting its strategic directions and organisational intentions. This involved filtering the University's goals throughout the organisation and to stakeholders in the wider community. The nine key cross-institutional goals included key performance indicators. Learning and teaching was identified as one of those key goal areas (USQ, 2012). The five key learning and teaching objectives focus on online innovation, enhancing the "student learning journey" and "best practice" blended delivery. Responsible stakeholders within the various faculties, as well as information and communication technology (ICT) staff and library staff, have the task of filtering USQ's priorities through to teaching staff with the underlying intention to optimise the student learning journey. USQ places particular emphasis on creating sustainable futures through activities that support communities and regions locally, nationally, and globally, and by USQ itself operating as a socially responsible organisation (USQ, 2009a, pp. 1 & 9). This understanding includes working towards "building Australia's skills base and progressing regional, national and global sustainability" (USQ, 2009a, p. 7). However, within the various key organisational documents at USQ, there are multiple understandings of sustainability. At the corporate level USQ aims for a "sustainability of market share" to ensure long-term institutional viability (USQ, 2009a, p. 17). In terms of USQ graduate attributes, "sustainability" is understood as positioning students to "meet the challenges of a rapidly changing world" (USQ, 2009a, p. 5). This requires academic staff to maintain up-to-date programs and course materials, and "prepare students for discipline expertise, professionalism, global citizenship, scholarship and lifelong learning" (USQ, 2009a, p. 14). In terms of learning and teaching processes, the word "sustainability" is understood to include quality improvement of USQ curricula and ongoing quality improvement of performance (USQ, 2009a). Strategic actions follow and include recommendations to embed the sustainability concept into programs and course materials, by building skills and knowledge relevant to indigenous perspectives, and through work-based learning, community engagement, and internationalisation of the curriculum.

Flexibility Principle

Likewise, there have been substantial changes in the area of flexibility in higher education. One in four Australian universities claims to be "flexible" (Universities Australia, 2012). Interpretations of flexible education have shifted the official meaning of flexibility in national education policy (Palmer, 2011) with Australian experiences of flexibility creating a "foggy mélange: external studies, extension studies, off-campus studies, open campus, open learning, flexible learning, flexible delivery, distance learning, distance education, correspondence learning, online learning, e-learning, etc" (Evans & Smith, 2011, p. 1). As a consequence, flexibility features in nearly every aspect of Australian higher education (Palmer, 2011). A Deakin University (2009) report for instance, argued many variables make the implementation of flexible education complex in practice. Although the literature has burgeoned in response, flexibility has, until now, been almost universally presented in uncontested ways. The Deakin University (2009) report provides some examples of these uncontested conclusions:

> Inherently better than other forms of education (Bigum & Rowan, 2004), as automatically leading to a more student-centred approach (Holzl, 1999) and as an unproblematic fix to perceived problems (Nicoll, 1997). (p. 12)

Further, in the Bradley (2008) review, references to flexibility can be "found frequently in conjunction with other adjectives that are intended to be desirable, for example, 'flexible and collaborative', 'flexible and adaptable' and 'flexible and innovative'" (Deakin Report, 2009, p. 12). This uncritical stance is emulated in higher education institutions which often include evidence of flexible practice in their strategic directions and teaching and learning plans. In terms of agreed best practice learning and teaching, flexibility is identified as being student-centred, using flexible learning spaces, and using more effective modes of knowledge transmission and flexible delivery of study materials (Commonwealth of Australia, 2008; Jones, Ladyshewsky, Oliver, Flavell, & Geoghegan, 2008).

Strategic Directions in Flexibility

Despite the literature on flexibility being largely uncritical, its impact is present in strategic responses made by the sector nationally and specifically at USQ. Whether it be a challenge from the Australian higher education community, from the Commonwealth of Australia, or from Julia Gillard when she occupied the Office of Australian Deputy Prime Minister and Minister for Education, Employment, and Workplace Relations (Commonwealth of Australia, 2008), being "flexible" is an escalating challenge for higher education institutions. Within the global university community, greater flexibility usually implies offering a range of different modes of flexible learning and supporting varied learning styles. For staff and the institution, it means employing strategies that enable them to teach via a range of modes and support multiple teaching styles.

USQ strategic directions have consistently embraced the notion of flexibility. In the first decade of this century, USQ was recognised as an innovator in flexible design and delivery of programs particularly in emergent pedagogical technologies and open courseware. In 1999, the International Council for Open and Distance Education awarded USQ the institutional prize of excellence for a dual mode institution, recognising the University's contribution in providing education at a distance to the world and its leadership and innovation in the field of distance learning. In 2001, then Prime Minister of Australia John Howard announced that USQ was joint winner of the Good Universities Guide's "University of the Year" for 2000-2001, recognising USQ's leadership in developing the e-University. Ten years later, USQ continued to position itself as "borderless" which is "broadly accessible, to a diverse range of students from a variety of locations" (USQ, 2009a, p. 3), embedding the term "fleximode" into policy and procedures (USQ, 2009b). By implication, no matter where a student is located, what their background is, or how busy they are, they can study effectively at USQ. They can be in Egypt, Germany, Hong Kong, or remote Australia, and the quality of the learning experience will be the same. USQ also expects that "flexibility principles" will be applied to assessment, ensuring responsive, innovative, and a range of assessment types (USQ, 2009b). Most recently, USQ strengthened this vision by establishing the Australian Digital Futures Institute (ADFI) which aims to research and develop innovative learning technologies.

Two Case Studies

We have discussed how the terms flexibility and sustainability apply at the corporate macro-level. Now we move to more micro-perspectives at the coalface to explore academics' understandings of two of the key principles of pedagogy. We draw on two sources of data: first, perspectives revealed in the survey of 54 international academics at USQ (see Chapter Six); and second, 2010 focus group data, as part of the SALT fellowship project (see Chapter Seven).

As outlined in Chapter Seven, international teaching staff shared their meanings of items in the SALT questionnaire. Of the 600 academic staff at USQ, one in six is international, born overseas with a language other than English as the primary language and where the higher education context and pedagogy are specific to a culture. Focus groups were conducted also to expose a set of interpretations and experiences in applying the five principles of tertiary pedagogy: Sustainability, Engagement, Scholarship, Flexibility, and Contextual Learning. The key intention was to build capacity and advance the ethical, sustainable and equitable teaching and learning practices of international academics. An unanticipated outcome of this research was that the academics provided insights into their understanding of the pedagogy expected of them.

During the focus group interviews, 15 international academics discussed the expectations, often implicit, they believed were fundamental to teaching in an institution such as USQ. Drawing from wide tertiary experience both in Australia and overseas, they expressed the desire to meet and excel in applying the USQ principles of best practice in learning and teaching, including those principles of Sustainability and Flexibility manifested in policy, committee structures and performance appraisals. That being said, many felt they were not ready to name the key strategic intentions of the University and those aware of the direction of the University sought clarification on a number of principles in the strategic plan.

Sustainability and Academic Staff

Data from the staff survey indicated a wide range of understandings of the concept of sustainability. As outlined in Chapter Six, the term had such diverse meanings that "sustainable" had become a catch-cry for phenomena considered "worthwhile". Despite the variations in responses, academics consistently referred to ethical knowledge and behaviours in explaining their responses to sustainable futures. Teachers in disciplines which must meet professional standards of ethical practice outside the academic environment had clearly defined understandings of the Sustainability principle. For example, Engineers' and Nurses' codes of ethical practice were taken seriously as academics readily identified ethics and privacy of online educational environments in the course they taught and in other courses in their faculty. The following quotes exemplify this:

> "*FET8611 provides some involvement with sustainable innovations in educational environments*"

> "*in nursing, the issues of ethical principles and ethical dilemmas in case studies encourage reflective thinking by nurses.*"

Some staff framed sustainability as preparing students for future changes to their professions, or as them helping students "to set their own goals", "to develop ethical practice in teaching and/or early childhood" and in "duty of care to patients in hospitals". Others expressed sustainability in terms of "commitment to lifelong learning; "ethics of people management"; "project managers answering multiple stakeholders"; "moral compared with legal issues in company practice"; "global warming and Sustainability in that context"; "teaching in a multi-literate world"; and "professional issues of bioethics and law". Thus, a broad range of understandings and experiences shaped their understanding of the pedagogical principle of Sustainability, and therefore the lens through which they interpreted the University's mission of providing sustainable futures in their teaching.

The international academics participating in the SALT focus groups critically described their understandings of the Sustainability principle. Defining the term caused confusion and affected their responses. One staff member wished to clarify the meaning of the term asking, "Does this mean what does Sustainability... actually mean in the lives of the students in their context?" Another mentioned that in her understanding, sustainability in a curriculum or a program context was "about longevity, it's about handing over, and it's about future orientation. In terms of a progression plan, progression policy for ensuring that the program is sustainable." Some staff were confused about what aspect of sustainability the University's senior administrators expected staff to address. Was it "academic sustainability, course sustainability, process and relevance sustainability, content and workplace sustainability?" Another educator thought it meant "how the learning process will be carried forward so that information is relevant and useable, future oriented." Another staff member sought clarification asking, "in terms of sustainability should we mention social, institutional and professional sustainability? In a way they are all interconnected."

Although a university's statements and principles provide a common benchmark for all stakeholders–including management, academics, students, and community–to understand its direction and intentions, they may not be interpreted the same way. Differences to the "shared or collective understanding" of the principles of Sustainability and Flexibility are evident across academic backgrounds and disciplines, posing challenges in designing quality learning experiences for students. Mixed messages on sustainability raise questions in academics' minds such as: "is what you are doing able to be maintained?"; "can the learners take it away once they finish the course with you"; "is it relevant to the real world....relevant for their future?"; "do the course materials and content have application to student's professional lives?"; and "does sustainability respect the local and regional contexts of the lives of our students?"

Another academic explained that "after the course I would get feedback from employers and industry. I have to ensure my course is relevant in the future and for my students when they graduate....because it's not just pertaining to ethics....it's also course stability (e.g., ensure technology and resources used in the course are relevant and are ongoing)." Another international academic felt a sense of uncertainty about the term "sustainability" and asked: "are we looking for more the 'ethical practice' of sustainability? Can we come up with a simpler definition: academic sustainability, course sustainability, process and relevance sustainability, content and workplace sustainability?" She suggested "as a staff member I will also be looking for a succession plan. I'm thinking that this is more about the content and the course being relevant in the future. It is about learning and teaching so continuity and sustainability of the content and the course is part and parcel of the sustainability of the course. We have to have a holistic approach here though to ensure the vision of sustainability is applied throughout the university. Maybe add course/program design. It is cross cutting all the courses and all the programs."

Flexibility and Academic Staff

In the staff survey (see Chapter Six), academic respondents generally indicated their understandings of the Flexibility principle in terms of their pedagogy. A sense of empathy with students was the highest priority. They aimed to maximise opportunities for students to learn effectively, given their diverse circumstances and settings. Examples included "developing ongoing presence on the StudyDesk that is encouraging and informative–aimed at giving the students a feeling of having a home base for that course and a feeling that they are not alone in their studies"; "making allowance for disability"; and providing "critical paths through the materials so that time poor students can engage with materials efficiently." Other significant aspects of teaching relied on providing clear objectives with meaningful constructive feedback on assigned work. Further, they recognised the need for balanced delivery across lectures, tutorials, online teaching, face-to-face and open discussion using ICTs, providing CD and online formats of quality course materials. The academics identified time as a factor that hindered their flexibility, as did the need for consistency in their teaching.

Mixed messages of staff understanding corporate expectations emerged. For example, one respondent said: "flexibility and support (are) not necessarily requirements of the course per se, but ....more about which courses they do, when and how well the university procedures can adapt to the sudden life changes that students often experience." Another pointed to a lack of flexibility at an institutional level as "the university is not flexible about due dates." One reflective academic, resigned to the need to adjust despite his frustrations about flexibility, accepted that: "in my opinion, USQ consistently fails to meet up to its own rhetoric with regard to inclusivity and flexibility–mind you, that still puts them ahead of many other universities."

In discussing the Flexibility principle, international staff participating in the focus groups understood this to mean "how things are delivered" and the many options and offers of courses at USQ. Their understandings were similar to those indicated from the staff survey results: "at this University so much of what we do is on the web as well as face-to-face as well as in printed material." Similarly, "flexibility is about whether you can access it in a different format," and "…for example, various modes, presentations, delivery and medium ….is there just a PPT, or is the PPT and audio as well as a written script for hearing impaired" (see Chapter Six).

The international academics believed the University expected them to be skilled in the online learning environment, as part of its emphasis on flexibility. Yet they felt inept at using ICTs: "it's still a dilemma for new IT." Newer academic appointees, in particular, were frustrated and anxious about "flexible learning environments". They perceived the pace of change was moving faster than they could address as individual teachers. Those who had been at the University longer were also anxious about changes expected of their practice. They had become competent at teaching external students using hard copy materials, as well as face-to-face teaching, but they now had to change again by offering a more "flexible" online delivery approach with a mix of resources and styles.

Summary: Mixed Interpretations

Review of academic literature and higher education policy and practice reveal the problematic understandings attributed to the Sustainability and Flexibility principles. We have identified one University's "official line" on these two concepts, which looks to embed the principles within its educational culture and practice. Results from the two case studies, however, reveal mixed interpretations and realisations of these two terms. Key University goals seek to support Sustainability and Flexibility principles at the macro-level, however, the way academics understand and apply these principles at a micro-level vary, in terms of their daily work and practices. Those teaching at the coalface thought flexibility refers to flexibility of teaching and learning options. But at the corporate policy level, it provides for a range of enrolment options–full time, part time, and three semesters–and decisions made at the administrative level about enrolment options to allow completion of a program.

A number of ramifications emerge because of this ambiguity and "mixed interpretations". At an institutional or macro-level, lack of clarity about the institution's key principles limits the "lived experience" of its vision and key statements. These include limitations on the quality control, efficiency, and optimisation of key principles of pedagogy. Staff may also perceive that adopting these principles in their daily practice is optional, which conflicts with the institution's goal to mainstream the guiding statements. The mismatch between messages and pedagogical practices filters down to students. They face inconsistency between what the institution promotes at a macro-level and what academics and support staff enact at the coalface.

A lack of consensus on key terms can significantly affect the health of staff by creating anxiety and feelings of vulnerability. Issues of inconsistency, inappropriate contextualisation of goals, in particular roles and practices, continue as there is misalignment between individual pedagogical approaches and the institution's direction and expectations. For example, Djordjevic and Cotton (2011) showed that the institution may want to convey a complex view of sustainability and its applicability to curriculum and pedagogic transformation, but recipients of the message understand sustainability as meaning turning off lights and using less paper in printing. The integrity of the message is highly likely to suffer in these circumstances, limiting the potential of the intended changes to behaviour.

Another ramification with this lack of clarity is the impact on promotional opportunities for staff, as their practices may not align with the institution's strategic directions and expectations. Lack of a systematic framework "limits quality control, efficiencies, recognition and sharing of good practices as well as lessons learned" (USQ, 2009c, p. 4). With reference to flexible delivery, USQ (2009b) advocates that a dispersed approach to the sharing of teaching and learning principles can dilute "the capacity to properly engage" with these principles and lead to perceptions about the adequacy of "infrastructure, tool sets and staff engagement and skills" (p. 4).

Conclusions

Mixed interpretations of key institutional guiding statements may make it unlikely for consensus on the meaning of the Sustainability and Flexibility principles. It is worthwhile to establish consistent messages on what key terms mean and how organisations will address them (Leal Filho, 2000). The final section of this chapter outlines a number of ways to help better translate organisational values and principles into culture and practices at a grassroots level.

Mainstream institutional teaching and learning principles must be clearly articulated to all stakeholders through transparent procedures which link policymaking to implementation. It is important for the institution to offer specific direction on how stakeholders are to define key principles and how they are to integrate, deploy, and promote them. For example, for staff to exemplify an institution's strategic direction and values, leaders must define key terms and tailor those terms to recipients' particular contexts and situations (Djordjevic & Cotton, 2011).

One way to improve clarity of the principles and key terms in organisational documentation is through a type of tool kit that includes exemplars and guidelines for best practice and consistent interpretation (USQ, 2009c). This process and set of resources could also include a range of self-guided professional development modules to increase staff confidence and understandings of these terms. As best practice, the guide could act as a reference point and draw on a range of innovative practices that staff already enact. Associated and relevant processes should also be introduced to help maintain consistency of institutional priorities, such as a checklist for academics on developing course materials and when communicating and collaborating with students (USQ, 2009c).

An institution's corporate vision, strategic plan, and core values should be central to staff induction and orientation processes. In addition, in-service training provisions on principles, such as Sustainability, need clarification for existing staff (Filho, 2000). The annual staff appraisal and review process could also incorporate opportunities for staff to demonstrate how they have integrated and actively engaged with these priorities within their teaching, research, and community engagement. The annual review process should also provide an opportunity for staff to request access to further support and resources (see Chapter Seven) that provides deeper understanding, skill development, and support in applying the key priorities in their pedagogy.

Staff can also be encouraged to provide examples of innovative practice, demonstrating how they have integrated and accounted for organisational key intentions within their teaching. In time, those ideas and practices could complement and be added to a repository of examples for new staff and those wishing to incorporate new pedagogical approaches. University learning and teaching awards could also recognise staff who have linked university direction with innovative practice and application. Leal Filho (2000) suggested that it may be strategic to set up working groups and network institutionally or cross institutionally to discuss how best to pursue specific initiatives on key terms and institutional principles. Senge (1990) had the vision of a "learning organisation" where "people continually expand their capacity to create the results they truly desire, where new and expansive patterns of thinking are nurtured, where collective aspiration is set free, and where people are continually learning to see the whole together" (p. 3).

It is important to actively promote key principles and institutional terms by clearly articulating the terms through consistent messages distributed in a variety of forms to promote institutional priorities systematically for all stakeholders. These messages would reinforce expectations about the University's commitment to, and ultimate increased application of, these five principles of pedagogy.

A Final Note

This chapter explored interpretations of the Sustainability and Flexibility principles in relation to contemporary theory and research. The chapter outlined ways in which these principles are promoted by the institution at the macro-level, and interpreted by staff at the micro-level. An organisation's guiding statements can cause ambiguity and mixed interpretations due to lack of an agreed definition or shared understanding. This has implications for various stakeholders as information filters throughout an institution. For a higher education institution to achieve its aim of a shared organisational vision, and to engage its academic community in that vision, consistency is called for in clarifying the meaning of terms, in mainstreaming the intentions of key principles–such as Sustainability and Flexibility–and in implementing processes that support the pedagogy.

References

Australian Council on Open, Distance and e-Learning. (2008). *ACODE benchmarks*. Retrieved from http://www.acode.edu.au/benchmarks.php

Bradley, D. (2008). *Review of Australian higher education - Final report*. Canberra, Australia: Australian Government.

Bonn Declaration. (2009). *UNESCO World Conference on Education for Sustainable Development*, 31 March -2 April, Bonn, Germany, pp. 1-6. Retrieved November 28, 2012, from http://www.esd-world-conference-2009.org/fileadmin/download/ESD2009_BonnDeclaration080409.pdf

Commonwealth of Australia. (2008). Review of Australian higher education. discussion chapter. Retrieved from http://www.dest.gov.au/sectors/higher_education/policy_issues_reviews/reviews/highered_review/default.htm#Review_of_Australian_Higher_Education_Discussion_Chapter_June_2008

Deakin University. (2009). *Perspectives on the future of flexible learning. Institute of Teaching and Learning*. Retrieved from http://deakin.edu.au/itl/assets/resources/persp-future-flexi-ed.pdf

Djordjevic, A., & Cotton, D. (2011). Communicating the sustainability message in higher education institutions. *International Journal of Sustainability in Higher Education, 12*(4), 381-394.

Evans, T., & Smith, P. (2011). The fog of flexibility: The riskiness of flexible post-secondary education in Australia. In E. Burge, C. Gibson, & T. Gibson (Eds.), *Flexible pedagogy, flexible practice: Notes from the trenches of distance education* (pp. 231-242). Edmonton, Alb.: Athabasca University Press.

Foster, J. (2002). 'Sustainability, Higher Education and the Learning Society', *Environmental Education Research, 8*(1), 35-41. Retrieved from http://www.tandfonline.com/doi/abs/10.1080/13504620120109637.

Gosper, M., Green D., McNeill, M., Phillips, R., Preston, G., & Woo, K. (2008). The impact of web-based lecture technologies on current and future practice in learning and teaching. *Australian Learning and Teaching Council, an initiative of the Australian Government Department of Education, Employment and Workplace Relations*. Retrieved 28 November 2012 from http://www.cpd.mq.edu.au/teaching/wblt/overview.htm

Growing Esteem. (2010). *The university plan 2011-2014*. Retrieved from Melbourne University website: http://growingesteem.unimelb.edu.au/growing_esteem/about

Jashke, K. (2007). DEEDS: The 'design education sustainability' project, first phase. *Research News,* Edition 17. Retrieved from University of Brighton website: http://artsresearch.brighton.ac.uk/news/deeds

Jones, S., Ladyshewsky, R., Oliver, B., Flavell, H., & Geoghegan, I. (2008). *Academic leadership for course coordinators: Results of a professional development program pilot.* Paper presented at the Teaching and Learning Forum 30-31 January, 2008, Perth, Western Australia.

Kennedy, M. M. (2006). Knowledge and vision in teaching. *Journal of Teacher Education, 57*(3), 205. Retrieved from http://jte.sagepub.com/cgi/content/abstract/57/3/205

Leal Filho, W. (2000). Dealing with misconceptions on the concept of sustainability. *International Journal of Sustainability in Higher Education 1(1):9-19.* http://www.esd.leeds.ac.uk/fileadmin/documents/esd/2._International_Journal_of_Sustainability_in_Higher_Education_2000_Leal_Filho.pdf

Moore, J. (2005). Is higher education ready for transformative learning: A question explored in the study of sustainability. *Journal of Transformative Education, 3*(1), 76-91.

Palmer, S. (2011). The lived experience of flexible education: Theory, policy and practice. *Journal of University Teaching & Learning Practice, 8*(3), 1-16. Retrieved from http://dro.deakin.edu.au/view/DU:30041161

Scott, G., Coates, H., & Anderson, M. (2008). *Learning leaders in times of change: Academic Leadership capabilities for Australian higher education.* Report of the Carrick Institute for Learning and Teaching in Higher Education, Strawberry Hills, NSW.

Senge, P. (1990). *The fifth discipline: The art and practice of the learning organization.* New York, United States Doubleday.

Sharp, L. (2002). Green campuses: the road from little victories to systematic transformation. *International Journal of Sustainability in Higher Education,* 3 (2) (2), 128–145. Retrieved 28 November 2012 from http://www.emeraldinsight.com/journals.htm?issn=1467-6370&volume=3&issue=2&articleid=839778&show=html

Sterling, S. (2004). Higher education, sustainability, and the role of systemic learning. In P. B. Corcoran & A. E. J. Wals (Eds.), *Higher education and the challenge of sustainability: Problematics, promise and practice* (pp. 47-70). Dordrecht: Kluwer Academic Press.

Thomas, I. (2009). Critical thinking, transformative learning, sustainable education, and problem-based learning in universities. *Journal of Transformative Education, 7*(3), 245-264.

Universities Australia. (2012). *University profiles.* Canberra, ACT: Author. Retrieved from: http://www.universitiesaustralia.edu.au/lightbox/1019

University of Southern Queensland. (2009a). *Strategic plan 2009-2013: Creating sustainable futures....embracing the digital education revolution.* Retrieved from USQ website: http://www.usq.edu.au/

—. (2009b). *USQ flexible learning framework.* Retrieved from USQ website: http://www.usq.edu.au/

—. (2009c). *USQ flexible learning: Executive summary.* Retrieved from USQ website: http://www.usq.edu.au/

—. (2010). *The university vision.* Retrieved from USQ website: https://policy.usq.edu.au/policy/files/university%20vision.htm

—. (2011). *The university strategy.* Retrieved from USQ website: http://www.usq.edu.au/aboutusq/strategy

—. (2012). *Learning and teaching excellence: Quality, policies, plans.* Retrieved from USQ website: http://www.usq.edu.au/

—. (n.d). *Quality management policy.* Retrieved from USQ website: https://policy.usq.edu.au/policy/files/Quality%20Management.pdf

Chapter Nine

Anticipating a Responsive, Relevant, and Agile Institutional Pedagogy

Jill Lawrence, Ann Dashwood, Lorelle Burton and Alice Brown

Introduction

This chapter reflects on the journey the research team undertook. It contextualises the journey against both the University of Southern Queensland (USQ) and Australian higher education imperatives, drawing out threads related to rapid changes such as technological innovation and managerial governance that are impacting on higher education. The chapter revisits the pedagogy to ask whether it embodies the capacity to be agile and relevant, able to respond to and accommodate change. As the journey ends the chapter asks: can the five key principles constitute the core of a whole-of-institution pedagogy that can accommodate the demands and challenges of the rapidly shifting contemporary higher education context? To answer this question, we revaluate and revitalise the principles in relation to the contemporary literatures underpinning them. They are also positioned against the various iterations of the USQ strategic plan to assess their viability in relation to USQ's mission, vision, and strategic directions.

This chapter considers key theoretical perspectives underpinning the journey: transnational education, best practice learning and teaching, and institutional pedagogy. USQ initially prioritised transnational education as its institutional vision in 2005, but by 2007, notions of flexibility and sustainability had taken its place. Transnational education has recently regained ground both nationally and globally, revitalised by calls for internationalisation of the curriculum. This supports its emerging relevance to Contextual Learning, one of the five key principles (see Crowther et al.,

2005). The theoretical nuances around the notion of "best practice" are also re-appraised.

Examining these theoretical perspectives provides the framework for the identifying argument of this book. If higher education institutions are to remain responsive, relevant, and agile in the rapidly changing higher education sector, they need to consider implementing an institutional pedagogy. This chapter will argue that an institutional pedagogy is indeed necessary for higher education institutions to prevail over the challenges confronting them. The five key principles–Sustainability, Engagement, Scholarship, Flexibility, and Contextual Learning–can together constitute a framework conceptualising the pedagogy.

The Five Principles Revisited

The first two sections of the chapter review the contemporary literature supporting the five key principles. The first section investigates the continued relevance of each principle in the Australian higher education context. The second section positions the revitalised principles against the current USQ Strategic Plan.

Sustainability Principle

Chapters Two and Eight explored various interpretations of the Sustainability principle, noting that academic research into sustainable teaching and learning practice is gaining momentum. Leal Filho (2011) observed that the theme has become a key developmental agenda item for more than 600 universities worldwide. Similarly, Kennedy (2006) noted that Australian and European universities were initiating research into what they see as an important aspect of teaching and learning. An impetus was the increasing realisation that in a globalising world, universities play a vital role in meeting the sustainability challenges of the future. The role of sustainability has likewise been expanded to introduce the idea of institutional approaches to pedagogy. The following section describes these initiatives.

Three main dimensions drive the view that Sustainability is a key principle in contemporary pedagogy: changing technological practices; interdisciplinary demands; and regional engagement. Rapid changes to our world, driven by technological advances, mean higher education graduates need to be flexible and creative. Intrinsic to this are multidisciplinary skills. Thomas (2009) argued that a transformative pedagogy underlies the extent of change, while others argue that students need to develop a range of analytical and context-related skills. To operationalise education associated with sustainability, teaching must focus on the processes of learning, rather than accumulating knowledge, to develop graduates who can improvise, adapt, innovate, and be creative (Thomas, 2009). Skills such as interdisciplinary thinking, problem solving, team working, and holistic thinking are critical. A pedagogy like problem-based learning (PBL) operationalises these skills, teaching students "how to think" rather than "what to think", within the framework of sustainability (Thomas, 2009).

A strand of the literature links sustainability to institution-wide practices. Thomas (2009) conceded there was a need for education associated with sustainability, but said the associated concepts and terms were contested: did this mean education for sustainable development, education for sustainability in general, or sustainable education practices? While education for sustainable development and education for sustainability represent increasing levels of change required in curricula, sustainable education practices require even greater change. According to Thomas (2009), a transformative pedagogy underlies the extent of the change, as more argue for students to develop a range of analytical and context-related skills. To operationalise education associated with sustainability, teaching approaches must focus on the process of learning, rather than just knowledge accumulation. That means developing graduates with capabilities to improvise, adapt, innovate, and be creative. Skills such as interdisciplinary thinking, problem solving, team work, and holistic thinking are often mentioned. The pedagogy of PBL encompasses these skills. PBL provides students with opportunities to learn to think, specifically "how to think" rather than "what to think," and potentially within the framework of sustainability. Consequently, identifying the commonalities of transformative learning, sustainable education and PBL is important. As universities begin to consider sustainability as a core value, a need emerged to link it to the role of transformative learning. Moore (2005) outlined three models of group learning–cooperative, collaborative, and transformative–in higher education. Moore also examined the implications of shifting university education toward a model for transformative learning and sustainability, introducing a number of questions for academics to consider. A key link here is critical thinking. Thomas (2009) argued that critical thinking skills are the key element in education about sustainability. The challenge is to transform pedagogy across the disciplines to enable academics and students to think critically.

Ties to community reinforce the view that Sustainability is a key principle in contemporary pedagogy. The context of where sustainability is instilled and ensured provides an interconnection with community so that it becomes specific to context, evolving, and open-ended (Jashke, 2007). As Chapter Eight revealed, views about sustainable practice reflected "a process of learning how to make decisions that consider the long-term future of the economy, ecology and equity of all communities" (Djordjevic & Cotton, 2011, p. 381). A focus on specific problems and particular solutions corroborates the idea that context is central–that sustainability suggests place-based and project-based approaches to student learning. USQ itself emphasises creating sustainable futures through activities that support "communities and regions locally, nationally and globally, and by USQ itself operating as a socially responsible organisation" (USQ, 2009, pp. 1 & 9). This understanding includes working towards "building Australia's skills base and progressing regional, national and global sustainability" (USQ, 2009, p. 7).

Sustainability's importance as a unifying educational principle is recognised nationally and internationally. The Bonn Declaration (2009, p. 1) for example stated that "we need a shared commitment to education that empowers people for change. Such education should be of a quality that provides the values, knowledge, skills and competencies for sustainable living and participation in society". Similarly, Vanderbilt University in the United States (Vanderbilt University, 2012) argued:

> The imperatives of sustainability point not only to a new course content, but also to new ways of teaching that content...as a project with relevance across the disciplines, sustainability presents a valuable paradigm for rethinking pedagogy. (p. 1)

The Australian Government's Department of Sustainability, Environment, Water, Population and Communities (2009) report called *Living Sustainably* outlined key principles. These included promoting learning which is interdisciplinary and holistic, and encouraging people to understand the complexities of issues threatening sustainability. The principles also included education incorporating: interdisciplinary and holistic learning; values-based, critical thinking; multi-method approaches; participatory decision-making; and locally relevant information, rather than predominantly national. The Australian Government Office for Learning and Teaching (OLT, 2010) report "Turnaround Leadership for Sustainability in Higher Education" contended that education and training were essential in developing sustainable practices in the way we live and work. The report introduced a project called Education for Sustainability (EFS) which aims to develop the knowledge, skills, and understanding required to make decisions thereby recognising the interdependence of our social, economic, and environmental systems. The goal of EFS is to empower individuals and communities to reflect on current practice, identify opportunities, and make informed decisions. Doing this requires a new way of thinking and a new approach to educational pedagogy.

As Chapter Eight noted, institutions can promote sustainability at the macro-level but staff and students must interpret it at a micro-level. An institution's guiding statements can cause mixed interpretations when there is no agreed understanding of meaning (see Chapter Eight). To implement a shared organisational vision, institutions must put in place mechanisms to ensure a coherent view of its expectations and consistent use of terms. These expectations are most appropriately met by an institutional pedagogy which prioritises Sustainability as one of its guiding principles. This is a contention that draws out a second key theme underpinning the chapter; that sustainability in these senses intersects with other key principles. While the Contextual Learning principle is explicitly mentioned in this section there are also the links to ethics and transformative and lifelong learning which foreshadow the Scholarship principle. First though the Engagement principle will be reviewed.

Engagement Principle

While literature on sustainability in learning and teaching is relatively recent, the literature on engagement is vast, substantiating its vital role in pedagogy. Student engagement involves activities and conditions likely to generate high quality learning (Australian Council for Educational Research, ACER, 2008). Engagement continues to be the focus of international and national surveys, such as the National Survey of Student Engagement (NSSE) in America and the Australasian Survey of Student Engagement (AUSSE), government reports (i.e., Bradley, 2008), and national research projects (Kift, 2009b; Kift, 2009c). The AUSSE (ACER, 2008) measures six engagement scales: academic challenge; active learning; student and staff interactions; enriching educational experiences; supportive learning environment; and work integrated learning. NSSE and AUSSE results suggest that engagement strategies enable students to normalise their learning experiences and reduce feelings of isolation and "otherness" (ACER, 2008). These frequently address issues such as: stress, uncertainty, and perceptions of inadequacy in a new academic environment; the "hit-the-wall" period when students realise the enormity of workload for the first time; and the lack of certainty about career choice so many school leavers experience. Government reports have also focussed on engagement. As Chapter Two noted, the Bradley Report

(2008) cited the word "engagement" 85 times. Other bodies such as the Australian Learning and Teaching Council (ALTC) and the Australian Office for Learning and Teaching (OLT) have commissioned national research projects on engagement.

The current research findings (see Chapter Three and Six) support the relevance of engagement. Both students and staff acknowledged the importance of the Engagement principle in the *Best Practice Learning and Teaching* surveys. Lawrence (2005) argued that students need to develop their own engagement strategies, including being personally assertive, asking for help, making social connections and expressing disagreement. Appropriate curriculum design can facilitate these skills. Many universities describe the graduate qualities or skills students need to develop to be successful in their future careers. The next section will argue that these skills comprise the essence of an institutional approach, albeit often from a marketing point of view. The research thus enhances the efficacy of an institutional approach encompassing carefully designed pedagogy to stimulate engagement in learning and teaching.

Scholarship Principle

Like engagement, the Scholarship principle is well established in the literature. As Chapter Two attested, scholarship of teaching involves academics engaging with research into teaching and learning and communicating in depth within discipline-specific contexts (Healey, 2000). McLeod, Tulloch, Ritter, and Kent (n.d.) added that teaching and research in higher education are highly interrelated. Research complements teaching by developing new theories, by injecting new knowledge about the learning/teaching process, by interrogating old theories and challenging assumptions, and by finding solutions to practical problems. Many scholars have argued that scholarship is a core ingredient of pedagogical inquiry. Hattie and Marsh (1996) suggested that marrying teaching and research by enhancing the relationship between them is a desirable aim of universities. Trigwell, Martin, Benjamin, and Prosser (2000) commented that scholarly teaching and learning are the core business of all our universities. This scholarly teaching perspective is discipline-specific, reflective, inquisitorial, responsive, and communicative (Trigwell et al., 2000) and underpins most models of scholarly teaching. (McCarthy, 2008) maintained that:

> Teaching is intellectual work, that student learning poses challenging problems that require careful investigation, that rich evidence about learning needs to guide thoughtful improvement and that the important

work of learning and teaching should not be allowed to 'disappear like dry ice' (Shulman, 1993) but be made visible, sharable and useful to others. (p. 1)

The proliferation of associations and academic journals dedicated to learning and teaching scholarship also testify to its key role in informing pedagogy (see McLeod et al., n.d.). These journals cover research areas such as PBL, action research, peer review, communities of practice, assessment, motivation, and diversity. A recent research strand stems from the need for tertiary institutions to demonstrate their achievement of learning and teaching outcomes (see Kember & Ginns, 2012). Funding agencies and government departments increasingly require tertiary educational institutions to demonstrate the benefits that such funding supports. This coincides with the prevalence of government assurance regulations and audits of university programs. Institutions must identify the goals, aims, or learning outcomes they are striving towards. They must also provide evidence that they have a teaching and learning environment that will help students achieve the stated learning outcomes. Furthermore, they must have a mechanism for "closing the loop"–demonstrating how they address any issues with students achieving the specified learning goals.

The review of the Engagement principle confirms its critical role in higher education pedagogy and also reveals its interaction with other key principles. That it intersects with Sustainability can be seen in the key role engagement plays in not only facilitating transition and retention but also lifelong and interdisciplinary learning, both of which are linked to sustainability. The next sections will outline how Sustainability and Engagement interact with Scholarship, Flexibility and Contextual learning principles.

Flexibility Principle

Like engagement and scholarship, there is a formidable literature on the flexibility in the higher education context. Not that there is agreement about its meaning. Palmer (2011) reported that conceptions of flexible education are changing, remaking the official meaning of flexibility in national education policy. Evans and Smith (2011, p. 1) argued that Australian experiences of flexibility have "created a foggy mélange." The USQ experience emulates this "fog". It previously was known as a leading external and distance provider, while its two latest strategic plans have prioritised online learning. Not that these views have marginalised Flexibility as a concept or a principle. Rather, according to Palmer (2011), the range of definitions means flexibility features in nearly every aspect of Australian higher education. As the Deakin University (2009) report argued the one certainty in the future is change: "There will always be new challenges and opportunities related to flexible education" (p. 5).

Others assert that flexible education is seen in Australia as a key institutional response to the many expectations placed on the modern higher education institution (Palmer, Holt, & Farley, 2010). Arguing that there can be no single model of quality teaching and learning for all student cohorts, Palmer et al. (2010) insist that a response of merely adding the online model to conservative models of traditional classroom and distance education forestalls genuine renewal. Palmer et al. (2010) call for coherent teaching and learning framework to achieve a set of "defined benefits" for defined student cohorts, "so that their course experience is one of learning environments and teaching strategies that are relevant, innovative, and responsive" (p. 76). The defined benefits they regard as more open, enriched, and active customised and personalised learning environments. A strategic frame of reference for creating differentiated, rich learning environments should guide and empower academic staff at the local level to deal with their realities–the disciplines, levels, ages, and locations of their students. In other words, the aim is for teachers to achieve fitness of purpose so that students realise the benefits (Palmer et al., 2010). Against this view, however, is the recognition that technological innovation provides the means for consistency within an institution. Learning management systems can be standardised, for example.

A recent focus in the literature is that related to personalised learning. A report written for the ALTC (Souter, Riddle, Sellers & Keppell, 2011) contends that previously the locus of technology was very much the teacher's domain, however, today's learners treat technology as integral to their learning-teaching relations. According to Souter et al. (2011, p. 9) the following aspects reflect perceptions of personal learning:

> Personal learning is an unlikely notion to traditional teachers, who are required to manage and attend to a large class of students. However, evolutionary turns in pedagogy and technology are shifting not only the locus of learning but also its focus (Nespor, 1994; Perkins, 2008). Recent decades have seen a move in the locations and intentions of learning away from classroom-based transmission to more flexible transactional exchanges and on to interactional communication over distances (Perkins, 1999). Whereas the traditional transmission focused environment located teacher and learners in an impersonal, highly structured institutional space, increasing use of technology has enabled and afforded greater flexibility (Oblinger, 2006). This flexibility has enhanced not only the physical environment and its arrangement but has also expanded the teacher learner

exchange further towards dynamic interchange whereby both teachers and learners are both learners and teachers, working together to further each other's understandings. (Savin-Baden, 2008b)

Thus the Flexibility principle not only constitutes a key principle in producing pedagogy but it is also beginning to enunciate a call for an institutional approach to pedagogy. An identifying characteristic of the principle is recognition that it is just that–flexible–and can accommodate change in both local and global contexts.

Contextual Learning Principle

The argument that Contextual Learning is a key principle in producing pedagogy is less emphatic. The data and ideas investigated in Chapters Five, Six, and Seven suggest that the literature on context is on one hand, limited and problematic, but on the other, a key ingredient in producing pedagogy. We support this view. That context plays a crucial role in pedagogy is a contention also supported by a number of theoretical perspectives.

Chapter Five argued that a growing body of industry and academic writing suggests that effective learning and teaching needs to be contextualised (Han & Singh, 2007; Reis & Kay, 2007) to support students who are learning locally and others scattered globally in a range of diverse locations. Context provides higher education institutions with an approach to achieve the authentic listening of voices and celebrating of difference (Cook-Sather, 2006). The greatest challenge for educators is knowing how to enable the student to tap into resources that maximise their potential for growth both as individuals and also as students engaged in learning journeys (Elson-Green, 2007).

Chapter Six foreshadowed that research literature on context included student-centred approaches to teaching (Prosser & Trigwell, 1999), social learning theory (Lankshear & McLaren, 1993; Lawrence, 2005), critical discourse theory (Gee, 1999; Van Dijk, 1996) and the literature exploring ideas about diversity (Devlin, 2009). It was argued that this literature sees human connection as a fundamental ingredient in the teaching/learning process. For example, Gee's (1999) ideas about diversity and discourses– or ways of knowing–suggest you can see students as a network of associations formed by their socio-cultural experiences. Appreciating the diversity of these "ways of knowing" in the classroom helps teachers to connect with students and acknowledge the complex influences they bring with them. Gee (1999) argued that pedagogy with too narrow a spectrum of diversity is impoverished: teachers need to continually shift their teaching and learning practices to accommodate diversity in their classes. The Bradley (2008) report reaffirmed the need for higher education institutions, especially regional universities, to consider diversity as the "status quo" rather than as a deficit. Lawrence (2005) referred to this shift as the deficit-discourse shift.

Like Flexibility, the Contextual Learning principle has an identifying characteristic. Its central and key role lies in interacting with the other principles. This stems from its capacity to enable each principle to fine tune itself to its context, whether a physical location, a technology, or an organising principle.

Dynamic Principles

As this review of the principles demonstrates, the principles do not function in isolation. They exist in a dynamic relationship with each other, intersecting and overlapping (see Figure 9.1). In a sector where change is a core ingredient and where there is little time for lengthy consideration before the next new innovation appears, for example, a sustainable approach is essential, whether in terms of forming a consistent university-wide approach to the adoption of a new technology or in terms of a learning design that takes into account both student and staff capacities in workload and resources. Interacting with the other principles, Sustainability assists an institution to be agile. Likewise Scholarship underlies the principles, as the principles would be limited in maintaining their applicability or their authority in changing times if they were not being informed and contested. Engagement also intersects with the others as an engagement strategy can only be relevant in a particular context or fine-tuned to a specific technology or learning and teaching strategy. Flexibility is also dynamic–the time and location of learning, the learning approach, the range of learning resources, and delivery and capacity of the learner to select when, how, and where to learn, require flexibility to actively engage students in learning. Finally, Contextual Learning also intersects with the other principles so that they remain relevant and fine-tuned to the context where learners and teachers engage each other.

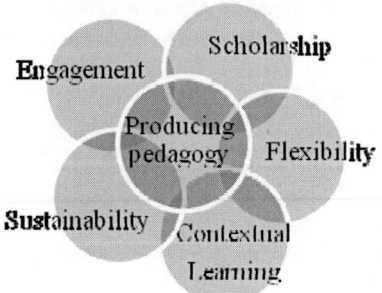

Figure 9.1: Intersecting principles in an institutional pedagogy

Summary

The literature review supports the argument that each principle remains relevant in the Australian higher education context, and worth being prioritised as a key principle underpinning pedagogy. While some of the principles are relatively recent, such as Sustainability, literatures underlying the principles of Engagement, Scholarship, and Flexibility are more clearly established in the literature. The five principles interact, intersecting with the others so that each enriches and enhances the others' applicability in the institutional context.

The next section positions the principles against the various iterations of the USQ Strategic Plan to assess their relevance to USQ's mission, vision, and strategic directions.

Strategic Planning, Best Practice Learning and Teaching

Most higher education institutions have organisational principles that describe "who they are and what they stand for". Two key organisational themes identified in the USQ Strategic Plan 2009-2013 were "flexible" and "sustainable" (USQ, 2009, p. 7). Thus USQ's vision changed from the focus on transnational education to an emphasis on sustainability and flexibility. The research team accommodated this change because of the continued relevance of the five principles–two of which were explicitly prioritised in the new vision (see Chapter Two). However, by 2010-2011, USQ had unofficially moved to "USQ Connected" with a "Digital First" vision. New staff appointments in the digital futures area instigated the shift but it was not supported or endorsed by a comprehensive document outlining mission, vision, or strategic statements. However, the technological imperatives implied in this vision coincidentally (or not) but explicitly prioritised the relevance of the Flexibility principle to an institutional approach to pedagogy, even if Flexibility as a concept was not clearly understood.

Table 9.1: USQ's Key Organisational Goals (2008-2013)

Organisational goal	Goal statement
Learning and teaching	To enhance teaching performance and to provide high quality, flexible and inclusive learning experiences that promote lifelong learning, critical enquiry and students' career opportunities.
Students	To create fulfilling learning experiences that are focused on student objectives.
Academic programs	To be recognised as a national leader in the provision of vibrant and contemporary programs responsive to the professions.
Research and research training	To be acknowledged leaders in applied research and research training, with a particular emphasis on research in sustainable futures.
Staff	To attract and retain excellent staff who exemplify USQ's values and provide them with opportunities to succeed personally, professionally and organisationally.
Educational partnerships	To maintain a profile of domestic and international educational partnerships that enhances USQ's position as a successful and leading higher education provider.
Social justice, equity and inclusion	To broaden equitable participation by students and staff and to encourage the development of a University culture that values diversity, multiculturalism and social inclusiveness.
Engagement and development	To derive mutual benefits for the University and its external stakeholders through engagement and development.
Enterprise	To deliver positive social, environmental and economic dividends.

Then, in 2012, with a new Vice Chancellor, USQ again revised its strategic plan and vision (2013-2020), supported by a comprehensive document. The 2020 vision is to be "to be recognised as a world leader in open and flexible higher education". The new mission is to enable broad participation in higher education and to make significant contributions to research and community development. USQ will achieve this while remaining a viable enterprise that: offers quality professional education opportunities that are accessible, flexible, and borderless; creates fulfilling experiences for all students based on the commitment of skilled and caring staff; develops graduates who are positioned to meet the challenges of a rapidly changing world; pursues world-class research, innovation, and practice in sustainable futures; and engages with communities, business, and government through ongoing and mutually beneficial partnerships. USQ's principal community contribution is to support Australia as a socially inclusive society, building its skills base and progressing regional, national, and global sustainability. USQ's competitive business advantage is to provide the highest quality educational experiences to students irrespective of their location or lifestyle. Table 9.1 outlines the USQ goal statements.

Summary

When USQ released its Strategic Plan 2009-2013, the two key organisational themes "flexible" and "sustainable" replaced transnational education. The research team accommodated this change in focus, examining both staff and students' perspectives of "best practice" in learning and teaching (see Chapters Three and Six). It is clear that the current USQ 2013-2020 Strategic Plan embraces all five key principles. While it explicitly refers to Sustainability, Engagement, Scholarship and Flexibility, Contextual Learning is also present, for example, through references to an "inclusive society" and "providing the highest quality educational experiences to students irrespective of their location or lifestyle". It is evident that recent literature galvanising transnational or international education also contribute to the rationale for the potency of the Contextual Learning principle (see Chapter Five). For example, the theoretical perspectives underpinning the principle of Contextual Learning challenge the notion of "best practice". The idea of one single "best practice" across different contexts becomes less appropriate. "Good practice" may be more apt, delineating practice that can adjust to differing contexts. We therefore contend that to comply with a "context effect", alternative terms such as "good practice", "most appropriate to the context practice", or "finely tuned" practice' may more appropriately replace the term "best practice".

This re-evaluation of the five principles and their positioning against the current USQ Strategic Plan validates their inclusion as grounding principles of pedagogy. The next section will revisit the theoretical and higher education perspectives renewing the concept of transnational education. The final section will address the question of whether, interwoven together, the principles can constitute the core of an approach to institutional pedagogy.

Transnational Education

In an unexpected twist, new directions in transnational education have provided another impetus for the role of context in an institutional pedagogy. The project chronicled in this book began in 2005 as a journey to uncover a transnational pedagogy. A promising research field, led by the University of South Australia and documented in Chapter One, was emerging. Many universities embraced the concept of transnational education as a framework for globalising learning and teaching practices. In Australia, transnational education and training–also known as offshore or cross-border education and training–was defined as the delivery and/or assessment of programs by an accredited Australian provider in a country other than Australia (Leask, 2004). This view of transnational education concurred with the Council of Europe's "Code of Practice in the Provision of Transnational Education" 2001 statement that transnational education incorporates:

> All types of higher education study programmes, or sets of courses of study, or educational services (including those of distance education) in which the learners are located in a country different from the one where the awarding institution is based. (Adam, Campbell, & Ottenwaelter, 2001, p. 13)

Differential applications of the concept of transnational education featured in the Australian university sector. Some institutions viewed it as an "established and integral part of the internationalisation activity" incorporating their university's local and global campuses (Leask, 2004, p. 5) while others understood it as mainly off-shore activities embedded within the culture of off-shore locations (Shoemaker, 2008). Both these views placed transnational education in the domain of institutional governance rather than an issue of pedagogy. Despite this, transnational education languished, a facet of Australian higher education taken for granted, uncontested, and uninformed by the literature. Some universities remain in this stalled position, still using general definitions that are over ten years old (Leask, 2008). Others have adopted more recent definitions or developed their own, a consequence of two major shifts in the higher education sector: the first in institutional governance and government policy; the second in pedagogical research. Each is discussed in turn.

Institutional Governance and Government Policy

A relatively recent transnational education phenomenon, alongside international branch campuses, is twinning and online education. Choudaha (2012) attributed these to the rise of "glocal" students, who seek an international education but want to stay local. This is a consequence of the growing consumer classes in Asia. According to Choudaha (2012) nearly 100 million people will enter the consumer class (annual income of more than $5,000) by 2015 in six south-east Asian countries–Indonesia, Malaysia, the Philippines, Singapore, Thailand and Vietnam–while between 2005 and 2025 China and India will see their aggregate urban consumption increase seven-fold and six-fold, respectively. Whereas international students traditionally go abroad for career advancement, quality of education, immigration, or the experience of living abroad, glocals differ as they look for career advancement and education quality without going too far from home. The needs of these students, combined with a changing institutional, demographic, economic and political landscape in an emerging Asia, calls for a new approach. Choudaha (2012) argued that internationalisation strategies need to move beyond student recruitment to target collaborative relationships of varying complexity, ranging from short-term exchanges to twinning international branch campuses. This presents a vital opportunity for foreign institutions to understand glocals and strategically engage them through innovative transnational education.

Both Australia's major political parties are grappling with the stimulus and opportunities that the growth of Asia and its middle classes provides. The Australian Government's (2012) initiative *Australia in the Asian Century White Paper* highlights the importance of international education in boosting productivity and links with Asia. The paper recommends that Australian leaders, workplaces, and institutions should become more Asia literate, with deeper knowledge and expertise of nations in our region. The Secretary of the Department of Foreign Affairs and Trade, Dennis Richardson, told a conference the government wanted more two-way flows of students. "The government wants to encourage students to be more language literate and better understand countries and cultures" he told a conference on China at the Australian National University (Lane, 2012). The Coalition Opposition meantime has recalled the 1950s notion of the Colombo plan which fostered the education of people from developing nations in our region. Called the Reverse Colombo Plan it will give more Australian based students the opportunity to study in an Asian nation.

These governance and policy issues coincide at another level. Student diversity and decreased funding support in the Australian higher education sector create an impetus for policy, educational, and research strategies in international education within Australian academe. The terms "internationalisation", "internationalisation of higher education" and "internationalisation of the curriculum" now found in most Australian universities' policy papers indicate the curricula needs of international students and Australian cultural diversity. International education and internationalisation of higher education are also important features in the United States, United Kingdom, Europe, Canada, and other nations. Governments and international organisations such as the United National Educational Scientific and Cultural Organisation (UNESCO) and the World Bank also use these terms (Clifford & Joseph, 2005).

There is also increased competition for academic staff. Kim (1996) suggested there is a new type of movement of academics crossing "borders at the same time as a new mode of knowledge production and the corporatization of the university on a global scale" (p. 398). The unprecedented expansion of the Asian tertiary education market has created growing competition for universities to attract the best staff from local teachers and further afield. This creates the need for a balance between retaining local staff and competing to recruit and attract international teachers (Hugo, 2008). International teachers are distinguished from local or "native teachers" in a number of ways. The literature includes terms such as "transnational academic mobility" (Kim, 2009) and "foreign trained teachers". It talks about cross-cultural differences in approaches to teaching, role expectations, and transitional adjustments in entering a professional learning environment from another country (Kuhn, 1996; Morgan, Appleton, & Sives, 2006).

Internationalisation of the Curriculum

Another of the shifts emanates from contemporary educational research. The term "transnational" has been reinvigorated in the term "internationalisation". According to Dolby and Rahman (2008), transnational education existed at the margins of educational research up until five years ago, but has now moved closer to its centre throughout the world. Some of these emerging research strands stem from governance issues. For instance, despite rapidly increasing student mobility, research has paid little heed to how students identify and mobilise abroad (Weiss & Ford, 2011). Focusing on the experience of Indonesians, Malaysians, and Singaporeans in Australia, Weiss and Ford (2011) explored how students understand their place, and the broader implications of globalisation and internationalisation for social and political activism.

Debates about public good versus commercial currency contribute to the rise in internationalisation. Joseph (2012) argued that the core missions of universities as knowledge creating institutions are education and training of qualified and specialised labour, research, and service to community. Universities also have the moral and social obligations of educating students to be democratic, caring, creative, and responsible citizens. However, Joseph (2012) also argued that the notion of universities providing a public national good as a valuable contribution to society has been eroded over the past decades. Education is now regarded as a commodity, a commercial product up for sale. Transnational education was embroiled in the debate because universities had to attract more full-fee paying international students to make up for growing budget deficits (Scott, Coates, & Anderson, 2008). Therefore, research in international education and internationalisation of higher education emerged from what began as a field of professional practices resulting from increased mobility of students (Dolby & Rahman, 2008). The focus moved to academic research on topics including markets and marketing, student satisfaction, international student learning, new models of pedagogy, intercultural relations, cost-benefit analysis, postcolonial relations with Asia, globalisation and educational aid, and flows of knowledge and cultures (Joseph, 2012).

The call for "global citizens" has generated further impetus for internationalism. This notion has risen in Australia in response to the demands of Asia's rapidly expanding middle class (Choudaha, 2012). The burgeoning need to equip Australian students with intercultural competency is strengthening this concept (see Lawrence, 2007; Leask, 2012; Mak, 2010). The prevalence in Australian higher education of graduate attributes which include global citizenship or intercultural competency further reinforces it. Another stimulus may arise from the discipline standards or Threshold Learning Outcomes (TLO) which Tertiary Education Quality and Standards Agency (TEQSA) may prioritise as its quality assurance measurement. The TLOs already developed invariably reference intercultural skills and competencies. Strategies to develop these graduate qualities have been focused on the formal curriculum, emphasising the development of a broad range of skills, knowledge, and attitudes. These include communicating and working effectively across cultures, the ability to think globally and consider issues from a variety of perspectives, awareness of one's own culture, and the capacity to apply international standards and practices within the discipline or professional area. A complementary focus on the informal curriculum–various extracurricular activities that take place on campus– has also recently emerged. Such approaches focus internationalisation strategies on all students, not just international students or Australian students who travel. Such approaches are typically flexible, creative, and clearly focused on internationalised learning outcomes. The goal is a student experience that prepares them for a rapidly changing and increasingly connected world, perhaps even to help solve some of the world's big problems.

The recent shift to revitalise transnational education highlights its relevance in explaining best practice pedagogy for the 21st century (Leask, 2012; Shoemaker, 2008; Thompson, 2003). Whichever view of transnational education a university espouses in policy and governance, the presence of international students inevitably involves staff in significant intercultural engagement with students and each other–whether the engagement is local, global, or *glocal*. The argument that transnational education is directed at *all* students is one that is gaining credibility in Australia. First there is the notion that internationalising the curriculum is no longer about just teaching international students (Leask, 2008). Rather, universities must change the curriculum for *all* students. As Leask (2008) argued:

> Indeed, increasingly in recent times the use of the terms 'international student' and 'domestic student', and the polarisation this suggests, is seen as obscuring the diversity within both groups and the need to focus on teaching all students well. (p. 1)

Second, as foreshadowed in the previous section, there is the recognition that internationalising the curriculum is connected with globalisation (Leask, 2008; Mak, 2010). With universities feeling a responsibility to prepare all graduates for a complex global society, they have been targeting graduate attributes related to internationalisation, again focussing on *all* students. A study the Australian Government OLT funded on the *Internationalisation of the Curriculum in Action* supports this view (Leask, 2012). The study found that differences in interpreting what an internationalised curriculum looks like is largely due to the different contexts within which the curriculum is designed and enacted. This includes such factors as institutional mission and culture, local professional accreditation requirements, the relationship between neighbouring nations in the region, and the discipline context. Thus the report recognises that the context is critical; that particular contexts shape and influence curriculum development or pedagogy.

The OLT report also identifies academics as key players in this process, reinforcing the notion that it involves a teaching principle (Leask, 2012). The study argued that in internationalising the curriculum, academic staff must work in program teams to critically review progress, confirm their rationale for further internationalisation, imagine new possibilities, and agree on an action plan for achieving their goals (Leask, 2012). Planning this sort of pedagogy might also include radically rethinking the program focus, introducing different types of learning and assessment activities for students, and providing opportunities for academic staff to develop their own international perspectives through collaborative research.

Summary

The notion of the Asian century has replenished and galvanised transnational education. The literature review suggests that it may be more appropriate to re-position transnational pedagogy as internationalisation. This shift has also impacted on our journey. In Chapter One we strived to visualise a transnational pedagogy. In this final chapter we argue that the revitalised view of transnational education, along with a repositioning of the five principles, has led us to reaffirm the efficacy of developing an institutional approach to pedagogy. The final section will revisit the concepts behind an institutional pedagogy.

Institutional Pedagogy

There is limited research literature exploring a whole-of-institution pedagogy in higher education. A much larger literature focuses on schools (Andrews & Crowther, 2003; Starratt, 2012). One strand stems from a school revitalisation initiative, the Innovative Designs for Enhancing Achievements in Schools (IDEAS; Andrews et al., 2011). The leader of the IDEAS initiative is Emeritus Professor Frank Crowther, the former Dean of Education at USQ. As documented in Chapter One, Frank began our journey with his goal of developing USQ's transnational pedagogy, using the IDEAS process as a model.

University mission and vision statements provide an impetus for an institutional pedagogy. These documents, almost by default, act as ad hoc holistic institutional approaches. This is an area that is not well researched however, despite the effort most universities put into developing their strategic plans. Many are led by marketing and corporate areas with academic divisions having little input. Literature, where it does exist, invariably expedites needs analyses documenting the various change forces impacting the higher education sector. Such strategic planning will guide institutional management, for example, the work of the sections and faculties often needs to explicitly provide links to or expedite the strategic plan. However, learning and teaching statements are not normally embedded in an encompassing pedagogy to accompany this strategic planning. The closest unifying strategy universities implement is through the graduate qualities or skills that students need to develop to be successful in their future careers. If these are mapped and aligned through programs/courses or degrees they could constitute unifying practices, though again not supported by theoretical perspectives. The new TLOs also offer this possibility, though at a discipline or program level not at the organisational level.

While literature on curriculum considerations linked to strategic plans is sparse, it is emerging. Clayton-Pederson and O'Neill (2005) moved from a focus on what they call "intentional learners" to developing "intentional institutions". They argued that technology makes the international institution more necessary as students' future careers require higher levels of education. For example, "education must enable individuals to discover what they need to know rather than just having static knowledge....society will need college graduates with mental agility and adaptability" (p. 3). According to Clayton-Pederson and O'Neill (2005):

> Colleges and universities are connecting silos of administrative work with relational databases so that, for example, financial aid structures can interface with human resources and accounting, ensuring students can work for the institution and maintain simultaneous student and staff categorizations. Eight years ago this was not easy, but today no one thinks it should be any other way. Clearly, technology can facilitate the achievement of the operational goals of the institution. But achieving one of its most important goals—improving the learning of all students— through technology will require conversations at all levels—department, college, institution, and state. With calls for greater accountability for increased spending and for assessment of student learning, we can ask for no less than the effective and coherent integration of technology into an

enriched curriculum that meets both student and societal expectations. (p. 15)

As discussed in relation to the Engagement principle, there are moves to implement institutional pedagogy at the first year experience (FYE) level. According to Kift (2009c), higher education literature has highlighted individual efforts to enhance the student experience, particularly in curriculum. But to be implemented fully, institutional players must better integrate their efforts. While explicitly addressing pedagogy in the FYE context, Kift's (2009b) arguments remain pertinent for a whole-of-institution pedagogy. Kift argued that institutions need to transcend the silos of academic, administrative, and support areas to enact a holistic vision for a student experience that is learning-focussed and greater than the sum of its many parts. This view concurs with Kift, Nelson, and Clarke (2010) and Tinto (2009) who argued that an institutional pedagogy might be significant in addressing student retention. While acknowledging the complexity involved, Tinto observed that student experience is one of the most widely studied areas in higher education. This has resulted in an ever more sophisticated understanding of the complex web of events that shape student leaving and persistence (Tinto, 2009):

> But for all that, substantial gains in student retention have been hard to come by... more importantly; research and theory have not been successfully translated into developing an effective institutional pedagogy. (p. 15)

In Australia, the need for an institutional response has intensified with the Federal Government's endorsement of Bradley's (2008) ambitious widening participation targets–that 40% of 25-34 year-olds should attain at least a bachelor-level qualification by 2025 (currently at 32% attainment) and that 20% of low socioeconomic states students should be enrolled in undergraduate higher education by 2020 (currently around 15-16%). This raises critical questions about the sector's pedagogical response. As the Federal Government identified in its vision, a positive student experience impacts on student transition, retention, and further study (Bradley, 2008). Improving the quality of learning, teaching, and the student experience, is critical in the success of universities and other higher education providers, both domestically and in the international market (Bradley, 2008). This is particularly important for adult learners who comprise a large proportion of students requiring additional support (Bradley, 2008).

Achieving the Australian Government's ambitious targets requires an increased emphasis on improving the student learning experience, to boost retention, progression, and completion rates. The question remains: how can higher education support, include, retain, and graduate student cohorts who will enter university with even greater diversity than ever before? Kift (2009b) argued that we must consider structural and cultural changes to the character of the student experience so that success is not left to chance. Kift (2009a) reconceptualised transition and argued that we need pedagogy which encapsulates the idea that:

> The curriculum and its delivery should be designed to be consistent and explicit in assisting students' transition *from* their previous educational experience *to* the nature of learning in higher education and learning in their discipline as part of their lifelong learning. The first year curriculum should be designed to mediate and support transition as a process that occurs over time. In this way, the first year curriculum will enable successful student transition into first year, through first year, into later years and ultimately out into the world of work, professional practice and career attainment. (p. 1)

This perspective reinforces the need for pedagogy which encompasses the whole undergraduate student experience–the academic, social, and support aspects as well as the extra-curricular activities on offer. Thus, the term "pedagogy" embraces a broader, holistic view of curriculum. This view incorporates the intentional design of learning, teaching, and assessment approaches that acknowledge the reality of the contemporary student context (Kift, 2009a). Specifically, pedagogy seeks to mediate the diversity in preparedness and cultural capital of entering students. Earlier views (see McInnis, 2001) did not encompass this whole-of-institution approach; rather they consisted of de-contextualised, "bolt-on" skills courses and disparate and "piecemeal" efforts to support the FYE (Krause, 2005) where engagement and retention are left to chance. They did not harness the curriculum as the academic and social "organising device"–as the "glue that holds knowledge and the broader student experience together".

Conclusion

Literature supporting the implementation of institutional pedagogy in higher education suggests two main themes. First, university mission and vision statements driving university strategic plans act as ad hoc holistic institutional approaches. This book, for instance, documents a journey that began in a pedagogical response to USQ's strategic mission. Such organising values or standards, though very rarely linked to research, foreshadow the role of an organising holistic pedagogy. Second, there are some emerging research and/or discipline areas that are beginning to identify the need for an organising and holistic pedagogy. From the FYE literature, Kift (2009a), Kift et al. (2010), and Tinto (2009) called for a transition pedagogy while Clayton-Pederson and O'Neill (2005) appealed for the development of intentional institutions to improve the learning of all students. Similarly, Senge (1990) visualised a:

> learning organisation where people continually expand their capacity to create the results they truly desire, where new and expansive patterns of thinking are nurtured, where collective aspiration is set free, and where people are continually learning to see the whole together. (p. 3)

This chapter has reflected on the journey the research team undertook, a journey made to perhaps anticipate just such a learning organisation. It began with the goal of developing an institutional pedagogy; a response to the University labelling itself as a leading transnational educator. Five key principles were designed to produce the core of the pedagogy: Sustainability, Engagement, Scholarship, Flexibility, and Contextual Learning. To test these principles, the research team undertook surveys to determine whether students and staff felt that USQ courses embedded the five nominated teaching principles. The team then undertook a USQ Fellowship, informed by the literature on the principles and data collected from the surveys. The Fellowship's purpose was to design and evaluate a professional development platform–Self-Assessment of Learning and Teaching (SALT)–to facilitate staffs' capacity to reflect on and enhance their learning and teaching practices. While the SALT platform is yet to be finalised, the longitudinal aspects of the journey galvanised the team to assess the impact of their journey to date. In particular, the team wanted to assess whether the principles could together produce a whole-of-institution pedagogy with an inbuilt capacity to remain agile, responsive, and relevant in a rapidly changing higher education context.

The project's longitudinal design caused setbacks generated by one of the themes of this book. This theme relates to the rapid globalisation and intense technological evolution creating massive and ongoing change in the higher education sector. Challenging assumptions about work, productivity, and an international demand for knowledge, skills, and resources, these forces ignite needs for highly skilled, knowledgeable, and culturally competent human capital. These demands are set against equity demands about wider access to higher levels of training and higher education for personal growth as well as demands to advance national goals of innovation and technology in a changing world. All this in a context where Government scrutiny and reporting is increasing, external quality audits are in place, and external pressures for change are escalating. Funding per capita is decreasing while competition is up; institutions are more commercial; students are more numerous, diverse, and forthright about getting value for money paid; and instances of litigation against universities are emerging. At the same time, rapid technology developments have made possible modes and approaches to learning unimagined 30 years ago. An increasing blending of various technologies, particularly digital, is used to deliver, manage, and support this education revolution.

This change interacted with our project in various ways. First, USQ's evolving strategic plan affected the project's identity: from transnational to best practice to personalised learning. These changes challenged us to re-evaluate the principles to ensure their alignment with both the University's and the sector's strategic directions. Second, the theoretical assumptions underlying each of the principles continue to evolve. Nevertheless, our project has found that the principles themselves remain relevant and salient in the higher education context. Likewise the interrelationships between the principles have continued to adapt and grow in response. Thus the impact of change in the sector not only confirms the need for pedagogy to be agile and relevant, the pedagogy must also respond to, and innovate in, the face of change. In turn, the five key principles have to be "change-able".

The chapter also revisited key theoretical perspectives underpinning the journey: transnational pedagogy, "best practice" learning and teaching, and institutional pedagogy. Transnational pedagogy has recently regained ground on both national and global stages, renewing its potency, in particular in the guise of internationalisation. This renewal underlies its newly envisaged role as a rationale supporting the Contextual Learning principle. The theoretical nuances of "best practice" were re-appraised to identify the relevance of the term "most appropriate to the context practice" to align with the re-visioned Contextual Learning principle. While the literature does not yet trumpet the call for institutional pedagogy, two themes foreshadow the importance of investing in this. University mission and vision statements act as ad hoc holistic institutional approaches while an emerging literature reveals support for pedagogy focussed in particular higher education areas. Such arguments could also be applied to the need for university-wide cohesive and holistic pedagogy.

The chapter's themes–our research journey, unremitting change, and theoretical perspectives–unify the book's fundamental argument. If universities are to remain responsive, relevant, and agile in the rapidly changing higher educational sector, they could consider unifying their teaching and learning practices through an institutional pedagogy. We purport that this pedagogy might have five key principles at its core– Sustainability, Engagement, Scholarship, Flexibility, and Contextual Learning.

References

Adam, S., Campbell, C., & Ottenwaelter, O. (2001). *The transnational education project report and recommendations*. Confederation of European Union Rectors' Conference. Retrieved from http://www.crue.org/espaeuro/transnational_education_project.pdf

Australian Council for Educational Research. (2008). *Australasian survey of student engagement. Australasia University executive summary report*. Retrieved from ACER website: http://www.acer.edu.au/ausse/reports.html

Australian Government. (2012). *Australia in the Asian century white paper*. Retrieved from http://asiancentury.dpmc.gov.au/

Australian Government Office for Learning and Teaching. (2010). *Turnaround leadership for sustainability in higher education*. Retrieved from http://sustainability.edu.au/news/article/turnaround-leadership-sustainability-higher-education-national-workshops

Andrews, D., & Crowther, F. (2003). 3-dimensional pedagogy: The image of 21st century teacher professionalism. In F. Crowther (Ed.), *Australian college year book 2003: Teachers as leaders in a knowledge society* (pp. 95-111). Deakin West, ACT, Australia: Australian College of Educators.

Andrews, D., Crowther, F., Abawi, L., Conway, J., Dawson, M., Lewis, M., Morgan, A., O'Neill, S., & Petersen, S. (2011). *Capacity building for sustainable school improvement: An Australian research study*. VDM Verlag Dr Muller, Saarbrucken, Germany. Retrieved from http://eprints.usq.edu.au/19101/

Biggs, J., (2003). *Teaching for quality learning at university: What the student does* (2nd ed.). Berkshire: SRHE & Open University Press.

Bonn Declaration. (2009). *UNESCO World Conference on Education for Sustainable Development*, 31 March -2 April, Bonn, Germany, pp. 1-6. Retrieved November 28, 2012, from http://www.esd-world-conference-2009.org/fileadmin/download/ESD2009_BonnDeclaration080409.pdf

Bradley, D. (2008). *Review of Australian higher education - Final report.* Canberra, Australia: Australian Government. Retrieved October 26, 2009, from http://www.deewr.gov.au/HigherEducation/Review/Pages/ReviewofAustralianHigherEducationReport.aspx

Choudaha, R., (2012). *Trends in international student mobility. WES Research & Advisory Services.* Retrieved from http://ihec-djc.blogspot.com.au/2012/03/new-report-trends-in-international.html

Cook-Sather, A. (2006). Sound, presence, and power: Exploring 'student voice'. Educational research and reform. *Curriculum Inquiry, 36*(4), 359-390.

Clayton-Pederson, A. R. & O'Neill, N., (2005). Curricula designed to meet 21st-century expectations. In D. G. Oblinger & J. L. Oblinger (Eds.), *Educating the net generation.* Colorado: EDUCAUSE.

Clifford, V., & Joseph, C. (2005). *Internationalisation of the curriculum: An investigation of the pedagogical practices at an Australian University.* Melbourne, Australia: Monash University.

Crowther, F., Behjat, N., Birch, D., Brodie, L., Burton, L., Connors, B., Cretchley, P., Dashwood, A., Hoey, A., Lawrence, J., Brown, A., Locke, J., Maroulis, J., Smith, A., & Wood, D. (2005). *Transnational pedagogy: A stimulus paper for consideration by the USQ professional community.* Unpublished manuscript, University of Southern Queensland, Toowoomba, Australia.

Dabner, N., & Davis, N. (2009). *Developing best practices in online teaching and learning to impact students and their organisations.* Paper presented at ASCILITE 2009 Conference. Retrieved September 1, 2010, from http://www.ascilite.org.au/conferences/auckland09/procs/dabner-poster.pdf

Deakin University. (2009). *Perspectives on the future of flexible learning.* Institute of Teaching and Learning. Retrieved from http://deakin.edu.au/itl/assets/resources/persp-future-flexi-ed.pdf

Department of Sustainability, Environment, Water, Population and Communities. (2009). *Living sustainably: The Australian Government's national action plan for education for sustainability.* Retrieved December 12, 2012, from http://www.environment.gov.au/education/publications/pubs/national-action-plan.pdf

Devlin, M. (2009). *How parents and partners can support student engagement.* Camberwell, Victoria: Australian Council for Educational Research.

Djordjevic, A., & Cotton, D. (2011). Communicating the sustainability message in higher education institutions. *International Journal of Sustainability in Higher Education, 12(*4), 381-394.

Dolby, N., & Rahman, A. (2008). Research in international education. *Review of Educational Research, 78*(3), 676-726.

Elson-Green, J. (2007). Looking beyond the Western perspective. *Campus Review*, p. 7.

Evans, T., & Smith, P. (2011). The fog of flexibility: The riskiness of flexible post-secondary education in Australia. In Burge, Elizabeth; Gibson, Chere and Gibson, Terry (eds), *Flexible pedagogy, flexible practice: Notes from the trenches of distance education* (pp. 231-242). Edmonton, Alb.: Athabasca University Press.

Gee, J. P. (1999). *An introduction to discourse analysis: Theory and method.* London: Routledge.

Han, J., & Singh, M. (2007). Getting world English speaking student teachers to the top of the class: Making hope for ethno-cultural diversity in teacher education robust. *Asia-Pacific Journal of Teacher Education, 35*(3), 291-309.

Hattie, J., & Marsh, H. W. (1996). The relationship between research and teaching: A metaanalysis. *Review of Educational Research, 66*(4), 507-542.

Healey, M. (2000). Developing the scholarship of teaching in higher education: A discipline-based approach. *Higher Education Research & Development, 19(2)*, 169-189.

Hugo, G. (2008). *The demographic outlook for Australian universities' academic staff.* Council for Humanities, Arts and Social Sciences (CHASS) occasional paper. Retrieved from http://www.chass.org.au/papers/PAP20081101GH.php

Jashke, K. (2007). DEEDS: The 'design education sustainability' project, first phase. *Research News, Edition 17*, University of Brighton. Retrieved from http://artsresearch.brighton.ac.uk/news/deeds

Joseph, C. (2012). Internationalizing the curriculum: Pedagogy for social justice. *Current Sociology, 60*(2), 239-257.

Kember, D., & Ginns, P. (2012). *Evaluating teaching and learning: A practical handbook for colleges, universities and the scholarship of learning.* Abingdon and New York: Routledge.

Kennedy, M. M. (2006). Knowledge and vision in teaching. *Journal of Teacher Education, 57*(3), 205. Retrieved from http://jte.sagepub.com/cgi/content/abstract/57/3/205

Kift, S. (2009a). A transition pedagogy for first year curriculum design and renewal. In *FYE Curriculum Design Symposium 2009*, Brisbane. Retrieved from http://www.fyecd2009.qut.edu.au/resources/PRE_SallyKift_5Feb09.pdf

—. (2009b). A transition pedagogy: The first year experience curriculum design symposium 2009. *HERDSA News, 31*(1), 3-4. Retrieved from http://www.herdsa.org.au/wp-content/uploads/herdsa-news-311-april-2009

—. (2009c). *Articulating a transition pedagogy to scaffold and to enhance the first year student learning experience in Australian higher education.* Final Report for the ALTC Senior Fellowship. Retrieved from http://www.fyhe.qut.edu.au/transitionpedagogy

Kift, S., Nelson, K., & Clarke, J. (2010). Transition pedagogy: A third generation approach to FYE–A case study of policy and practice for the higher education sector. *The International Journal of the First Year in Higher Education, 1*(1), 1-20.

Kim, Y. Y. (1996). *Becoming intercultural: An integrative theory of cross-cultural adaptation.* Thousand Oakes, CA: Sage.

Kim, T. (2009). Transnational academic mobility, internationalization and interculturality in higher education. *Intercultural Education, 20*(5), 395-405.

Krause, K. L. (2005). Serious thoughts about dropping out in first year. *Studies in Learning, Evaluation, Innovation, and Development, 2*(3), 55-67. Retrieved from http://sleid.cqu.edu.au

Kuhn, E. (1996). Cross-cultural stumbling blocks for international teachers. *College Teaching, 44*(3), 96-99.

Lane, B. (2012). Colombo plan redux. *The Australian higher Education Supplement*, July 4. Retrieved from http://www.theaustralian.com.au/higher-education/colombo-plan-redux/story-e6frgcjx-1226416071072

Lankshear, C., & McLaren, P. (1993). (Eds.). *Critical literacy; Politics, praxis and the postmodern.* Albany: State University of New York Press.

Lawrence, J. (2005). Reconceptualising attrition and retention: Integrating theoretical, research and student perspectives. *Studies in Learning, Evaluation, Innovation, and Development, 2*(3), 16-33. Retrieved from http://sleid.cqu.edu.au

—. (2007). Two models for facilitating cross-cultural communication and engagement. *International Journal of Diversity in Organisations, Communities and Nations, 6*(6), 73-82. Retrieved from Common Ground Publishing website:

http://ijd.cgpublisher.com/product/pub.29/prod.423

Leal Filho, W. (2011). Applied sustainable development: A way forward in promoting sustainable development in higher education institutions. In W. Leal Filho (Ed.), *World trends on education for sustainable development*. Frankfurt: Peter Lang Scientific Publishers.

Leask, B. (2004). *Transnational education and intercultural learning: Reconstructing the offshore teaching team to enhance internationalisation*. Australian Universities'Quality Agency (AUQA) Occasional Paper. Retrieved from: http://www.auqa.edu.au/auqf/2004/program/papers/Leask.pdf

—. (2008).Internationalisation, globalisation and curriculum innovation. In M. Hellsten & A. Reid (Eds). *Researching international pedagogies: Sustainable Practice for teaching and learning in higher education* (pp. 9-26). Springer: The Netherlands.

—. (2012). *Internationalisation of the Curriculum in Action.* Final Report for the OLT National Teaching Fellowship, Retrieved 30 October 2012 from http://www.olt.gov.au/resource-internationalisation-curriculum-action-2012.

Mak, A. S. (2010). Enhancing academics' capability to engage multicultural classes and internationalize at home. *International Journal of Teaching and Learning in Higher Education, 22*(3), 365-373.

McCarthy, M. (2008). The scholarship of teaching and learning in higher education: an overview. In R. Murray (Ed.), *The scholarship of teaching and learning in higher education* (pp. 6-15). Berkshire: The Society for Research into Higher Education and Open University Press.

McInnis, C. (2001). *Signs of disengagement? The changing undergraduate experience in Australian universities*. Melbourne: CSHE. Retrieved March 4, 2009, from http://repository.unimelb.edu.au/10187/1331

McLeod, S., Tulloch, M., Ritter, L., & Kent, J. (n.d.). *A few practical tips and a useful survey of higher education associations and journals in publishing. Scholarship in teaching and learning.* Retrieved from http://www.csu.edu.au/division/landt/reschol/documents/mcleodpaper.doc

Moore, J. (2005). Is higher education ready for transformative learning: A question explored in the study of sustainability. *Journal of Transformative Education, 3*(1), 76-91.

Morgan, W., Appleton, S., & Sives, A. (2006). Should teachers stay at home? The impact of international mobility. *Journal of international Development, 18*, 771-786.

Palmer, S. (2011). The lived experience of flexible education: Theory, policy and practice. *Journal of University Teaching & Learning Practice, 8*(3), 1-16. Retrieved from http://dro.deakin.edu.au/view/DU:30041161

Palmer, S., Holt, D. & Farley, A. (2010), Towards new models of flexible education to enhance quality in Australian higher education. In D. Kennepohl & L. Shaw (Eds.), *accessible elements: teaching science online and at a distance*. Edmonton: AU Press, Athabasca University.

Prosser, M., & Trigwell, K. (1999). *Understanding learning and teaching: The experience in higher education*. Buckingham: Society for Research into Higher Education & Open University Press.

Ramsden, P. (2003). *Learning to teach in higher education*. London: Routledge.

Reis, N., & Kay, S. (2007). Incorporating culturally relevant pedagogy into the teaching of science: The role of the principal. *Electronic Journal of Literacy Through Science, 6*(1), 54-57.

Senge, P. (1990). *The fifth discipline: The art and practice of the learning organization*. New York, United States: Doubleday.

Shoemaker, A. (2008). *If the world is our campus, where are we going?* Retrieved from http://www.monash.edu.au/teaching/passport/chapter/html

Souter, K., Riddle, M., Keppell, M., & Sellers, W. (2010). *Spaces for knowledge generation*. Sydney, Australia: Australian Learning and Teaching Council. Retrieved December 12, 2012, from http://documents.skgproject.com/skg-final-report.pdf

Starratt, R. J. (2012). *Cultivating an ethical school*. London: Routledge.

Scott, G., Coates, H., & Anderson, M. (2008). *Learning leaders in times of change: Academic leadership capabilities for Australian higher education*. University of Western Sydney: Australian Council for Educational Research. Retrieved 26 October, 2012, from http://research.acer.edu.au/

Thomas, I., (2009). Critical thinking, transformative learning, sustainable education, and problem-based learning in universities. *Journal of Transformative Education, 7*(3), 245-264.

Thompson, E. (2003). New partners in learning: An effective teaching and learning framework for offshore students. In *Partners in Learning. Proceedings of the 12th Annual Teaching Learning Forum, 11-12 February, 2003,* Perth, Edith Cowan University. Retrieved from http://lsn.curtin.edu.au/tlf/tlf2003/abstracts/thompson-abs.html

Trigwell, K., Martin, E., Benjamin, J., & Prosser, M. (2000). Scholarship of teaching. *Higher Education Research & Development, 19(2)*. Retrieved from http://www.itl.usyd.edu.au/projects/scholarshipproject/about.htm

Tinto, V. (2009). Taking student retention seriously: Rethinking the first year of university. In *FYE Curriculum Design Symposium 2009*, Brisbane. Retrieved March 4, 2009, from http://www.fyecd2009.qut.edu.au/resources/SPE_VincentTinto_5Feb09.pdf

University of Southern Queensland. (2009). *Strategic plan 2009-2013: Creating sustainable futures....embracing the digital education revolution*. Retrieved from http://www.usq.edu.au/learnteach/qualpolplan/plans

Vanderbilt University. (2012). What is sustainability? *SustainVU*. Retrieved from http://www.vanderbilt.edu/sustainvu/who-we-are/what-is-sustainability/

Van Dijk, T. A. (1996). *Discourse as social interaction.* London: Sage.

Weiss, M., & Ford, M. (2011). *Temporary transnationals: Southeast Asian students in Australia.* Journal of Contemporary Asia, *41(2),* 229-248.

ABOUT THE AUTHORS

Professor Lorelle Burton is Associate Dean (Learning and Teaching) in the Faculty of Sciences at the University of Southern Queensland (USQ). Registered as a psychologist, Lorelle has received multiple local and national teaching excellence awards. She has authored market-leading first year Australian psychology textbooks and heads national research projects on factors that impact on student learning. Lorelle currently leads USQ collaborations with community groups promoting community capacity building and well-being.

Associate Professor Jill Lawrence is Associate Dean (Learning and Teaching) in the Faculty of Arts at USQ. Jill's research on learning and teaching in higher education and enhancement of the student and staff experience led to the award of an inaugural national ALTC citation with Eleanor Kiernan and an individual Australian Carrick Award for Teaching Excellence in 2007. Jill has served on institutional and faculty learning and teaching committees and assessed national teaching excellence citations and grants.

Dr Ann Dashwood is a Senior Lecturer in Applied Linguistics & TESOL in the Faculty of Education at USQ. Accepted into the USQ Teaching Academy for teaching enhancement of TESOL in higher education contexts, she now supervises doctoral candidates in the broad discipline of Applied Linguistics. Across the Languages and Cultures Network for Australian Universities (LCNAU) Ann contributes as a teacher-researcher in classroom discourse and second language learning and teaching.

Dr Alice Brown is an educator with 25 years' experience in early childhood, primary and tertiary settings. She is recognised by her peers for innovative practice, leadership and teaching excellence through learning and teaching awards and fellowships and as an invited member of the USQ Teaching Academy. Alice presents and publishes in the area of learning and teaching in Higher Education and was a finalist in Lecturer of the Year 2009.